COUNTRYWOMEN ON THE LAND

Memories of Rural Life in the 1920s and '30s

G.K. NELSON

ALAN SUTTON

For Irene

First published in the United Kingdom in 1992 by
Alan Sutton Publishing Ltd · Phoenix Mill · Far Thrupp
Stroud · Gloucestershire
First published in the United States of America in 1992 by
Alan Sutton Publishing Inc. · Wolfeboro Falls
NH 03896–0848

British Library cataloguing in Publication Data

Nelson, Geoffrey K. (Geoffrey Kenneth) *1923–*
Countrywomen on the Land
I. Title
942.009734

ISBN 0–7509–0181–0

Library of Congress Cataloguing in Publication Data
applied for

Cover picture: Mowing the Hay, 1920 (Brooks)

Typeset in 11/13 Bembo.
Typesetting and origination by
Alan Sutton Publishing Limited.
Printed in Great Britain by
The Bath Press, Avon.

CONTENTS

ACKNOWLEDGEMENTS

In addition to the major contributors whose names appear at the beginning of the relevant chapters, I should like to thank those other contributors whose words are quoted elsewhere or who have allowed me to use the photographs they have sent. There are a few photographs – mainly postcards, which I have purchased at sales and whose origins are not known to me. I apologize to the photographers whom I have not been able to contact and if they get in touch with me, I shall be pleased to acknowledge their work in any future editions.

The following contributions are thankfully acknowledged: Mrs Ann Powers, Walpole, Norfolk; Mrs Irene Anderson, Ketton, Stamford, Lincolnshire; Mrs Borrett, formerly of Depwade, Norfolk – present address not known; Miss Brett, Diss, Norfolk; Mrs Sheila Graver, Wrexham, Clwyd.

Photographs have also been supplied by: Mrs Brooks, Mr Park, Mrs Stacey, Mrs Toulson, Mrs Bye, Mrs Ellington, Mrs Newling, Mrs Poole, Mrs Wallis, Mrs C. Betts, Mrs S. Dobson, and the Editor of the *Daily Mirror* who has given permission to publish photographs.

I am also grateful to Mrs M. Sparks who helped with the collection of material, to Mr and Mrs E. Kemp. who helped with the transcription and typing, and to Mrs I. Nelson for proof-reading and for her general support.

INTRODUCTION

As we grow older there is a tendency to look back to the past and when I retired I decided to devote time to collecting material that related to the period of my childhood and youth in the 1920s and '30s.

I was born and brought up in the heart of rural Norfolk and lived in a world that is almost totally alien to the world we live in today. In those days few villagers travelled further than their nearest market town, with perhaps a visit to the seaside at Wells or Great Yarmouth on a day trip. As far as agricultural workers were concerned the only paid holidays they got were Christmas and bank holidays, and it was only in 1939 that they gained the right to a week's holiday. Country people still lived in isolation, gaining knowledge of the outside world only through newspapers, radio and visits to the cinema.

Life centred on the family and the village community. Women may have had less contact with the outside world but the life of the family and of the community centred around them. In this book we view the world through the eyes of a number of ladies who have given accounts of their experiences.

I have used the word 'ladies' deliberately because it was the approved usage in that period of time, though today I find the term is often rejected in favour of the word 'women', largely because of an assumed social class difference between women and ladies.

Before the Second World War the distinction was made on the basis of what may be called moral status rather than class. My mother and grandmother were the wives of farm workers, but they considered themselves to be ladies and they described all their friends and other females of whom they approved as ladies. The highest praise they could bestow was, 'She is a real lady.' On the other hand they described those of whom they disapproved as 'That woman.'

There was undoubtedly a social hierarchy in the villages that to some extent cut across the usual barriers of social class, at least at the level of the workers and farmers of smaller holdings. The barrier between this group and the wealthy farmers and landowners was seldom breached but we are concerned in this study with the great majority of country folk, whether on the farms or engaged in other employment; with the small farmers and tradesmen; and, in this particular book, with their wives and daughters.

My grandmother and mother never worked on the land although grandmother had been a domestic servant before her marriage. How common this was I am not sure but it seems to have been the aim of most men to be able to support their wives and families without the need to send them out to work.

Certainly the role of women was seen, by themselves as much as by men, to be 'home-makers'. They spent their time in domestic work, including the care of children. Of those who were forced by economic circumstances to work, the majority seem to have undertaken domestic work for local farmers. The daughters of farm workers were often employed as domestic servants by wealthy local families or by farmers. Indeed, one of my informants said that as a condition of his employment, his daughter was required to work as a domestic servant for the farmer who employed him.

The daughters and wives of farmers with small farms often worked beside their menfolk. And many farm workers' wives were employed on the land, particularly for seasonal work such as potato picking, fruit picking and during the corn harvest. Women were also often employed in the dairy and oversaw the care of poultry. They were paid less than the men, even when doing the same kind of job, and were thus exploited as a cheap source of labour, but all these matters are explained and described more clearly in the words of the ladies who have contributed to this book.

When I set out to undertake a study of life in the first half of the twentieth century, I appealed for information through the columns of local country newspapers and received over three hundred replies. Some of these contributions from male farm workers were published in a previous book *To be a Farmer's Boy*, but the contributions received from the ladies were reserved to provide the basis for the present volume. I have had great difficulty in selecting which items to include and have attempted to do this in such a way that the material used gives a representative picture of life in different parts of the country as seen through the eyes of those who experienced it. While in this introduction and my conclusion I have brought together much of the information from informants whose material I have not been able to publish at length, this work consists of first-hand accounts by contributors which I have edited for publication. The material has come to me either as handwritten accounts or as material recorded on tape. As far as possible the contributors speak for themselves and their distinct personalities are apparent in what they have to say. In this way we are able to arrive at a clearer understanding of the society in which they lived and to get a feeling of participation in a different and, indeed, a lost way of life.

Over the years many women writers have described their experiences of country life. Some of these authors are rightly remembered but others have unjustly been forgotten. Two of the best-known authors were Flora Thompson and Alison Uttley.

Flora is best remembered for *Lark Rise to Candleford*, a combination of earlier books published in 1945. She was born in Juniper Hill, a small settlement in Oxfordshire, on 5 December 1876. Her parents were Albert and Emma Timms.

She attended the village school in Cottisford and after leaving school at the age of fourteen, she obtained work as a clerk in the post office at Fringford. After a number of moves to various post offices, she finished up at Grayshot where she met John Thompson whom she married in 1903. Thompson was also a post office clerk and in that year he obtained an appointment at Bournemouth post office and it was in that town that they began their married life. In 1916 John was moved to Liphook where they lived until 1928 when they moved to Dartmouth. Flora lived here until her death in 1947.

Flora's descriptions of country life, based on her own experiences, are unmatched in country literature, except perhaps by writers such as Richard Jefferies and Alison Uttley.

However, I have also been inspired in preparing this work by a number of other women writers whose works, while less well known, should be recommended to the reader.

Mollie Harris' book *From Acre End* (1986) gave me the idea of presenting individual contributors' stories in their own words. Her book, which is the story of the Oxfordshire village of Eynsham, brings the society of the village to life through this method of presentation. Her book *Cotswold Privies* (1984) has a fascination all its own.

Susan Hill's book *The Magic Apple Tree* (1982), takes us on a delightful trip through a year in the country, as does Annette MacArthur-Onslow's *Round Houses* (1975), which is also beautifully illustrated by the author.

Betsy Whyte's *The Yellow on The Broom* (1979), helps to counter-act the prejudice against 'the travelling people' that is still very common in this country.

I must refer back to an earlier period and mention the three works by Marthena Blomefield that give a very detailed story of life on a Norfolk farm in the 1880s. These are *The Bulleymunge Pit* and *Nuts in the Rookery*, which appeared in 1946, and *Bow-Nets and Water Lilies* which came out in 1948. They were all published by Faber.

In this book I have tried to give a number of ladies the opportunity to tell their stories, All of these will help us to understand a very different way of life and a culture from which we still have much to learn.

Romance in the harvest field, from an old postcard

CHAPTER ONE

RURAL LIFE IN BUCKINGHAMSHIRE

Mrs Phyllis Tibbetts, who was born at the beginning of the twentieth century, gives a lively account of her experiences of life on a farm in Buckinghamshire during the first three decades of the century.

In 1909 my father took a job as a farm bailiff on a private estate. His wages were £1 per week. The head gardener and groom were paid the same. All had a rent-free cottage with a large garden, a can of milk each day and a pound of home-made butter every week. The daymen and boys only got 10s. per week (50p today).

It was there I first remember the haymaking. Every year seven men used to come in to scythe the meadows as in those days machines were not in use. They all wore white striped shirts and velvet cord trousers. These were hitched up a little and either had a leather strap or a piece of string round them just below the knee. This was to give the men freedom to bend a little as they scythed so they did not have to keep stopping to hitch their trousers up. They did a swathe each all the way up the field, then turned and did the same coming back. The same team of men hired themselves out to anyone who needed them. They were very cheerful and always sang or whistled as they worked.

My mother always made them cans or jugs of tea three or four

Mrs Tibbetts working with her father haymaking at White Hawridge Farm, Chesham, Buckinghamshire in 1924 times a day. They had lunch at 10 a.m., dinner at 12.30 p.m. and a snack in the late afternoon. Lunch and the snack were usually bread and cheese with an onion or apple. Dinner was often the top of a cottage loaf with a big piece cut out of the middle, that was usually filled with a big lump of boiled bacon which they ate by cutting a piece of bread off and a piece of bacon bit by bit. They called it a 'thumb-bit'. When they spoke of food they mostly called it 'vittles' or 'bait'. Sometimes they brought a very long pasty for their mid-day meal. The wives made them with meat at one end and fruit or jam at the other end. As a child I was fascinated to see them cut them in half at meal times. They usually brought them in a big tin wrapped first in greaseproof paper and then in a damp cloth so that the food did not get too dry in those hot summers. The people they worked for usually gave them a quart of beer or cider with their dinners.

Around 1912 I saw a mowing machine for the first time. It was an ugly-looking thing made for one horse. It had a very wide central wheel with a seat over it, and a long pair of shafts for the horse with the knife driven by the wheel on one side. The pull of the knife was rather a disadvantage as it often caused the horse to have a sore shoulder on that side. That invention did not last long. The next mowers were made for a pair of horses, a long pole between them and a bar at the end to strap to their collars, and the chain traces were fixed to whipple-trees for pulling – these were level and did not cause sore shoulders. The knives were longer for quicker mowing which was a big advantage. These mowers also had a seat for the driver but as there were no springs it was a shaky, bumpy drive. In those days the hay was turned and dried by hand. Once it was dry it was put into heaps, which we called 'haycocks'. As a rule there was just enough to be picked up cleanly with a pitchfork to load on the wagon. The hay was carted and stacked loose. There were no balers in those days. When it was required for use a small amount of thatch was pulled off and the hay was cut out in chunks of about three foot by two foot and about two foot deep. If it was for use on the farm the men would carry that chunk on a pitchfork to the cattle yards, sheds or stables. If it was for selling it was put on a weighing machine and each truss had to weigh fifty-six pounds. It was then tied very tightly by two strings. Odd trusses at the farm were 1s. 6d. (7^1/2p) or £3 per ton. Straw was £1 per ton, and so were swedes and mangolds. Good quality oats and wheat or barley were about £5 per ton. Fresh milk was 1^1/2d. per pint and 1s. per gallon (5p). Best farm butter was from 1s. 3d. to 1s. 6d. per pound, skimmed milk was 2d. a quart and eggs 10d. per score (twenty).

The cottages where my maternal grandparents lived were a row of three all with huge gardens and big sheds. Half-way down the gardens was a very pretty little house. Actually it was the place shared by the three cottages to do the washing, baking, pig curing and so on. It was brick-built with lattice-paned leaded windows and a tiled roof. There were two large rooms. The first one you entered had a very strong, long bench under the window, a big bread oven in one corner and a large copper (a real copper) in the other corner. Between them was a big chimney for smoking the bacon. There was also a huge wooden tub about six or seven foot by three foot and about three foot deep. That was used for scolding and cleaning the pigs after killing and also for salting pork and bacon. The other room had strong shelves along one side that used to be used to store cheese to ripen. In my day it was often used to hang up the washing on wet days, or to do the ironing. There was a large brick-built tank, lined with cement, outside the wash-house where rain-water caught on the roof was stored, handy for the copper or the tubs.

The cottages were fairly typical for farm workers of those days. There were two rooms downstairs both with brick floors. They had quite good sized rooms as families were usually large. In the living-room there was a very wide fireplace. It had an open fire, with an oven at one side and a water boiler on the other. The boiler had a lid in the top for filling it and a brass tap at the bottom to let hot water out. On each side of the fireplace there were seats where us

Mrs Tibbetts, manageress of a farmshop owned by The Hon. H.E. Eaton, 1933

children loved to sit in the winter. There was a cupboard on the window side of the fireplace with shelves above where Gran's 'best' china was kept, which was only used on Sundays, birthdays and at Christmas, etc.

The stairs went up from what was called the 'back house'. There was a big cupboard under the stairs where Gran kept her everyday china, pots, pans, cooking utensils and the big red bread pan. There was a food cupboard and one for brooms, brushes and tools, with a high shelf where Grandpa kept his powder and shot for his muzzle gun, and the caps and cartridge cases that he used to refill, as well as the little machine that was used to turn the ends of the cartridges in after they were refilled.

There was no sink and the washing up was done in a big tin bowl on the table and drained on a big tray. The used water was carried across the lane and thrown away, except if it was very dry and water was short, then every drop was saved for the garden. There was no water laid on in those days and the only supply was the big rain-water tank. The water caught on the roofs went through a charcoal filter before it reached the tank. That tank was shared by the three cottages for drinking, cooking and cleaning in the house, every drop drawn up by a bucket suspended by a clip hook at the end of a long wooden pole. You can imagine the work. There were no mod cons at all, just oil stoves for extra cooking or summer-time when it was too hot for a fire, and oil lamps or candles for lighting.

We mostly used wood for fuel. All the summer we went wooding as often as time allowed. Dead wood from the trees in the orchard was sawn out and saved, and we were allowed to have any fallen branches from the trees or the chips when the workmen felled any trees. The thin branches were tied into bundles called 'faggots'; these were stored in the woodshed to dry and used for fire lighting and the fire under the bread oven where a whole faggot was put in at once. The thicker branches were sawn into logs. Those too big for a handsaw were sawn by a long cross-cut saw which had handles both ends and was pulled back and forth by two people. Then these were split by an axe and stacked in the wood-shed to keep dry for winter. We always said they warmed us three times: once fetching them home from the woods, as they were carried home on our backs or shoulders, and the very heavy branches we put a rope round and dragged; twice when we sawed them up; and again when we sat by the fire in the evenings.

Life was very full every day, yet we really enjoyed it. Money was short but love was plentiful. Our parents were firm but also kind.

There were no buses in the country then. Our village had three carriers who drove into High Wycombe two or three times a week. They had wagonettes or vans with long seats facing each other at the back. You could ride into town for 3d., if you could afford it that is. We usually walked, though if we had a very heavy load of shopping to bring back the carrier would cart it for 1¹/₂d.

My father had a bicycle and every Saturday he rode into Wycombe to buy the meat. In those days you could get a big leg of mutton for 2s. or a large hand spring of pork for the same price. Brisket of beef, salt or fresh, was 1¹/₂d. a pound, and we usually had twelve pounds for 1s. 6d. Mother would bone and roll it and use the best part to roast for Sunday dinner and the rest was boiled with the bones and lots of vegetables and big fluffy dumplings. A flank of bacon (belly) was the same price. We usually had twelve pounds every week. The best streaky was boiled, used hot for one meal, and the rest used cold. The other end which was not so lean, was sliced up to fry with bread and eggs for breakfast. In the winter we often cooked swedes and an onion with the boiled bacon, and turnips in the summer; both were very tasty. Bread was 2d. a loaf. In those days a large loaf weighed about two-and-a-quarter pounds. A small loaf cost a penny farthing.

We were brought up on some good old maxims: 'Honesty is the best policy'; 'Waste not want not'; 'Do unto others as you wish them to do to you'; 'Take care of the pennies, and the pounds will take care of themselves'; and many similar sayings.

We said our prayers at our mother's knees at bedtime. We also went to Sunday school and church, though the church was two-and-a-half miles walk each way.

Our school was a Church school, and we had a little service before lessons and grace before and after lunch for those who stayed, and many did because that school served several scattered hamlets and farms. Many children walked three or four miles to school. Our vicar came to the school every week riding on a very ancient bicycle. He was very fond of children and we all loved him. When he came there was always a big rush, the big boys to push his bicycle and the younger ones to hold his hands or his coat if they could get near enough. He was not a remote figure who only spoke in church on Sundays but a dear friend to all the villagers. Occasionally we had non-Christian pupils and they would come to school at 9.30 when the service was over and in time for the register. What we learnt, we learnt with such thoroughness that I can remember it all even now, and I started school in 1911.

Even at school there were no mod cons. Water was from a pump, but was still rain-water. The toilets were primitive buckets. There were oil lamps and one tortoise stove in each room; it was very cold in winter. Mother used to send us to school with a hot jacket potato in each pocket to keep our hands warm. We left them in our pockets to eat at morning playtime. Of course there were no school dinners in those days, but our teachers would always make us a hot drink if we took cocoa or Oxo, and we were allowed to eat round the fire provided we left everything clean and tidy.

We played outside in all weathers except heavy rain – vigorous games to keep us warm in winter and quieter ones in summer. If the boys fell out they would fight, but it was not a free for all – the boys had to fight it out with a ring of us all round to see fair play. When it was over it was handshakes all round and no nastiness.

We had great love and respect for all our teachers and there was never any unruly behaviour. The headmaster had a cane and used it if he had to. It was not often needed.

There was a policeman in the next village who, like the vicar and church, served both villages. He rode around on a tall bicycle. We called him 'Old Daddy Chambers' but not to his face of course, and not in a nasty way either as we had quite a good liking for him. He was strict but fair.

If any of us got into bad mischief, and at times we all did, he would come to the school, give us a stern lecture and say, 'This has got to stop. I've warned you and if I catch any of you doing that again you will get a taste of my belt, and that's not a threat, it's a promise. It is no use my giving you a summons, that would only punish your parents who would have to pay for your wrongdoing and you would not feel it. But believe me if you feel my belt you won't forget it.' Then he would thank the headmaster and stalk out.

The boys were very fond of throwing stones at the white china cups on the telephone poles and they often hit them and broke so many that the police were told. That was one thing we got warned about. My brother was one of the culprits who got caught, and he got the belt as promised, and when he went howling home to mother, she said, 'Serve you right for being so destructive.' We were not encouraged in wrongdoing.

There was no crime at all in our area and seldom any in the country. With policemen like 'Old Daddy Chambers' to keep order, it was no wonder. Yet he was really loved by us children and highly respected.

'Waste not, want not' was not just a maxim – it was a dire necessity in those days, and nothing at all was wasted. Sheets were turned sides to middle when they got thin, and when they got even more worn the best parts were cut up for pillow-cases or nappies. The worst parts were put in the first aid drawer to use for pads, for ointment poultices, or bandages. You doctored your own ailments if possible; the doctor was only called in the most dire necessity.

Old suits, coats and trousers were washed and cut up for rugs; no one had carpets. The cottages had brick, tile or stone floors downstairs and these thick rugs were very good for keeping your feet

warm. We had lino in the bedrooms, and made rugs for the bed-
side, washstand and dressing table. When they got dirty they were
washed in a big bath and put through the mangle and dried. They
lasted for years and usually we made them round the fire on winter
nights. Mother would look out for pretty garments at rummage
sales to help make them. She also looked out for evening shirts, and
would use the backs of them to make pillow-cases, as ordinary people in the country never used such things. You could often get
three or four for a penny. She used the fronts and sleeves for han-
kies, properly made with hem stitching. I can still remember
pulling the threads for her. She had been a nanny before she married and would not have anything makeshift or shoddy. She would
also look for garments of good quality that she could cut up to
make clothes for her children, so we were always well dressed. Dad
did not drink or smoke and we had a much nicer home, clothes
and food because of that.

All the surplus fruit was made into jams and jellies for the winter
and a lot was bottled. You seldom saw anything tinned, and fridges
were unheard of.

Potatoes, carrots, swedes and turnips were clamped to keep for
winter. They were put into an oblong heap with the sides made to
slope, covered with a thick layer of straw and then a thick layer of
earth. At the top of the ridge they usually let in two pieces of pipe
for ventilation to stop the vegetables from sweating as that could
cause them to rot. A trench round the clamp was made when we'd
dig out the earth to cover the clamp, and that allowed drainage that
kept the clamp dry. Of course, it got filled in again as the vegetables
were used. Any swedes or turnips left in the late spring were set in
a trench across the garden and when they made new growth we
used the tops for cooking like greens. They were delicious.

Onions were hung on string to dry; the small ones were used for
pickling. We made pickled cabbage, piccalilli or mustard pickle and
pickled mushrooms, walnuts, gherkins, plain mixed pickles and nasturtium seeds, as well as all sorts of chutneys – apple, marrow,

plum, gooseberry and many more. Onions were also used in sick rooms, cut in half and laid in saucers of water, before disinfectants came into general use. I can remember that being done up to the 1914 war.

Herbs were used for ointments, hand-creams and so on – usually with a base of lard which, of course, was home-made when we killed the pigs. Blackcurrant cordial was freely used for colds and children were given a few tablespoonfuls in a glass or mug of hot water. Elderberry syrup was used for the same reasons and as a tonic. Raspberry and gooseberry vinegar were used for bad chests. 'Cutting a cold' they called it and cut it certainly did as both were sharp enough to cut anything.

Elderflowers were used for ointments, creams and lotions, and were excellent for the skin. Stinging nettles were a splendid tonic and blood purifier and we used them in several ways. In spring we always picked them when they were young for cooking, and if that was done properly you couldn't tell them from spinach. We also made stinging-nettle tea and beer which we stored in bottles, so we had a tonic all the year round. Dandelions are another good source of iron and we used them a lot in salads and sandwiches. They need to be picked young as the old leaves get very bitter. Nasturtium seeds and leaves are also very tasty in salads. My Gran had a lovely herb garden and made all her own remedies.

In those days every village had its craftsmen – builders, carpenters, wheelwrights, blacksmiths, thatchers and hay tiers (who usually worked piece-work for anyone who needed them). Our village thatcher could thatch houses, barns, churches, lych-gates or porches, as well as stacks, and did really beautiful work.

There were usually several carriers and often a herbalist. We had one in our village. He not only collected herbs for most of the chemists for miles around but made good remedies himself and people went to him before they went to a doctor. He could cure most things but if he was uncertain, he would make sure you went to a doctor. I earned my pocket money collecting herbs for him until well into the 1920s when he died and was very greatly missed.

There were also several men that we called 'Bodgers', who worked for themselves. They usually had a hut in the woods, or near their home. The one near us had a big thatched hut beside the lane near our cottage. The Bodgers used to buy beech wood straight from the woods. This was cut into lengths and then split into strips about two or two-and-a-half inches square. These were then stacked high to dry and season and kept under a shed or thatched shelter until they were ready. Then they were made into chair legs which were turned on a lathe worked by one foot. I used to spend hours watching him when I was a child. The chair legs were done piece-work for the chair factories in High Wycombe. He used to give us the chips and shavings for the copper fire that heated the water on wash-day or for baths. He was a craftsman and could make the most lovely furniture. His mother was a lacemaker, as were a lot of village people, including my mother. They made the lovely Buckinghamshire Pillow lace.

The art of making home-made butter with all the lovely patterns on it has died out. I know dozens of patterns, not done with moulds but with the butter pats. Another craft was patchwork.

It was not all work though. We had our flower shows, concerts in the village hall and schools, whist drives and dances, cricket in the summer and football in the winter and games at home indoors on winter nights. We used to play cards, dominoes, draughts and chess and mother often read to us.

There were Sunday school and church outings and sports meetings between the villages, as well as an Annual Dinner for the farmers, gamekeepers, earth stoppers and any other ordinary people who helped with the hunt. My father, who did not drink of course, was a very welcome guest as he was often the only one fit enough to see the ones who had over-indulged safely home, as it meant a long walk from the station with no transport available. It was often hilarious and Dad used to tell us funny stories about it afterwards.

Most employers on large estates gave a big party for their staff
and all the children, where for one day in the year they waited on
the staff instead of the other way round and they gave us all a wonderful time. A huge dinner with plenty to drink, presents for everyone from a big Christmas tree and everyone who was old enough
was asked to do something to amuse their fellow guests. My
Mother was very good at reciting and Dad would sing and play the
violin fairly well. The groom and head gardener could sing too.
Mother generally taught me a little poem to say.

I can remember that I first heard a gramophone at one of these
parties before 1914. It had a large horn and when it blared out
quite near me suddenly, I was so scared I cried and it was years
before I could be persuaded to listen to a gramophone again.

I remember too, the large shooting parties on the big estates,
sometimes with King Edward VII and later King George V being
present. These days came to an end with the war of 1914–18 and
the world has never been the same since. Men went to the slaughter in thousands every day.

Morals deteriorated badly; it was no longer 'honesty is the best
policy' in many cases but rather 'every man for himself'! Children
grew up without their fathers, often without any discipline or
guidance as their mothers were working. Rudeness crept in and
good manners went out and those who were lucky enough to have
their fathers return from the War hardly knew them and often
resented them. Many women had found a new independence that
they were loath to give up and some had also been unfaithful to
their husbands so many homes broke up. That left a lot of men
more disillusioned than ever, especially if they had kept faithful to
their wives.

Many people went bankrupt during the War, and men came
back to find estates and farms sold and their jobs gone. There was
no unemployment pay for farm workers and many found themselves on the verge of starvation. In fact, in our village in the 1920s,
some people did die from starvation. Many people lived on parish

relief which was barely enough to keep body and soul together.

There were always some tramps on the roads even before the First World War, but after it was over, there were even more – it was pitiful to see so many. My mother had a heart of gold and would give to all who called, though she could ill afford to. Mostly she gave them something to take away and a bottle of tea or some tea and sugar and a small tin of condensed milk. Dad was not so soft hearted and he used to grumble at times and say, 'They know you're a soft touch, and tell each other where to come. You shouldn't encourage them.' Mum would say, with tears in her eyes, 'I can't help it Tom. If I turned one away it might be the very one who really needed help badly, and we are not short of food. I can't and don't give money. I know how they must feel.'

One tramp was very independent and he always insisted on doing something for his food, like sawing some logs, mending a fence or cleaning the windows. He became a friend for life. He was an old regular soldier, straight as a lance and spotlessly clean. His eyes were very bad, so he could not get a job. Mum told him any time he was down and out to come to us and he did. When mother died I told him to come to us which he did all his life. He would never come in the house, but in his last years I made him a room in what used to be an incubator room. It was nicely lined and had a window and I gave him a camp-bed and mattress, bed clothes and pillow, and he was very glad of a little comfort in his last years. Today he would have been looked after and at least had Social Security. There were many tramps right up to the Second World War.

One came up the drive of the big house where we worked. My husband and I ran the farm side of the estate then. We were leaning on the fence after tea watching the young chicks. The tramp asked the way to the house and did we think the boss would give him a shilling or two. We knew he was not likely to get help there and said so. The tramp said he was trying to get a few pence to pay for a night's 'Doss', as he called it, at Old Windsor Workhouse. I gave him some food and a jug of tea, and my husband gave him half a crown (12¹/₂p today). He was so pleased he could not thank us enough and said to my husband, 'If you want to get your money back with interest, you back April 5th in the Derby. I've been sleeping rough where he's in training and I've seen and heard what's going on. They expect him to win, but do him each way just in case. He's a right outsider and will be a good price. You do as I say and you will be repaid.' So all of us who worked on the estate and in the house had our humble shilling each-way on April 5th. Of course, there were no betting shops in those days and taking bets was more or less illegal. There were people who did it on the quiet and one of the fellows who worked there said he would get our bet on for us. He put them on with a man who ran a small coal business. Whether or not he thought the horse had no chance and would not win so did not hedge the bet, I do not know, but I remember it took him weeks before we all got our money.

During the 1920s there was still much unemployment and dreadful poverty. One winter at threshing time three unemployed men came to help with the threshing. One to clear the straw, which in those days was tied up in bundles; there were three bundles to a truss which weighed fifty-six pounds. Another man had to clear the cavings; these were the grassy stalks too short for straw which came out at the side of the drum. The third man looked after the chaff bags. The chaff had two outlets on the side of the drum, so that when one bag was full that outlet could be shut and the other sack filled. While that was being done the first sack was taken off, tied up and carried to the barn, where it was stored with the cavings for feeding the animals. In those days nothing was wasted. These poor men were so weak and under-fed they found the work, light as it was, more than they could manage. Mum gave them food and a hot drink for the mid-morning break, and a good hot dinner. But after lunch they had to give up. I had been on the rick throwing the sheaves on to the drum, but with the loss of three helpers we

15

Mrs Tibbetts going to work at 6 a.m., 1928

were in a fix, so Mum came out and went on the rick and I had the job of clearing the straw, cavings and chaff on my own, which kept me very busy, but I did it. So from that you can tell how weak these poor men must have been.

I often think we are getting too far away from nature, and nature has a way of getting back at us if we do. I was amused when I saw in a newspaper that someone was disgusted at a mother breast-feeding her baby in public. When I was young nearly everyone did so, wherever they were. If the baby needed feeding, the baby was fed indoors or outdoors, in the hay field or on the train, and no one took any notice. In fact, no more notice than we did of a cow suckling a calf, a ewe with her lambs or a cat with kittens.

I often wonder if many children born with brain troubles or deformities are partly caused by the drugs they give to pregnant women. I never saw many children like that years ago, at least in the country. During the Second World War I was asked if I would give pony rides to the children at a Mental Hospital on their fête day, because with petrol shortages the fair they usually had could not get there. There were hundreds of little spastic children. It was a great success and I did it for many years.

Another thing that amuses me is the way today people talk of organic farming, just as if they have discovered something new. In my young day there was nothing else, all farming and gardening was organic. Everything that came off the farm was put back into the land. The animals were fed the hay, corn, chaff and cavings, the seeds, mangels and kale. The pigs had the small potatoes, skimmed milk, middlings, barleymeal and oatmeal. We crushed our own oats by hand, turning the handle manually and very hard work it was too.

Only the best long straw was kept for thatching; the rest was used for bedding for the animals and a little for the cattle yards, and every bit went back onto the land. That kept the bulk of the soil which cannot be done by using chemicals. Every field had its hedges and trees to shelter it, and there was no danger of soil erosion as the manure kept the moisture and bulk in the soil, instead of making it a dust bowl.

I am appalled at the way most farmers farm today. I call it factory farming. They have cut down the trees and grubbed up the hedges, not only spoiling the beauty of the countryside but also gradually destroying our environment.

The unnatural conditions they keep animals and poultry in would never have been allowed when I was young. Stables, cow-sheds and pigsties were inspected and every animal had to have a certain amount of space for its comfort.

I have spoken out against keeping hens in batteries since it was first thought of in the 1930s. They say outdoor poultry does not pay, but I know different, as all my life I have kept poultry. Up to 1978 I was still keeping free-range hens. I don't say we got rich but we made a good living. I am not very popular with some farmers for I have often said, 'No one is entitled to deprive any of God's creatures of fresh air and sunshine. I only wish I could make you live in the same conditions you make your animals live in, and see how you liked it.'

During the First World War, tractors began to appear on some farms, but where we lived we did not use them as they were easily turned over on the steep hills. In many places the old steam ploughs were still in use. They had two big engines, one each end of the field, and the plough was pulled back and forth between them. They could plough eight to twelve furrows each. The plough had two sets of shares, one for each direction, so that when they had gone across the field the man who rode on the plough pulled a lever which tipped up the across plough shares and set the return ones. I still recall watching them as a child. It was quite a business when they moved from farm to farm. The two great engines pulled the iron plough, the men's living hut and the huge steel cables. You can imagine the noise on the narrow roads made of flint as all the wheels were made of iron. You could hear them coming for miles, which was just as well if you had a horse and cart or were riding. It gave you a chance to find a place to pull in out of the way when it was too narrow to pass, and not many horses liked to face those monster engines. I give the drivers their due, they were very considerate if there was a horse about, and would go as slowly as possible and try to make less noise.

Another rural job was that of the stonebreakers. They sat beside the roads, a heap of huge flint stones on one side of them, which they broke one by one with a hammer to make them a suitable size for remaking or mending the roads. They sat with a sack over their shoulders if it rained or was cold. When it was warm they sat with their jackets off and their sleeves rolled up, but always with a thick sack or two over their knees to protect their trousers from the sharp flints. The roads were a great hazard to us as children because if you fell you usually cut your hands or knees badly. They were bad for bicycles too; those sharp flints easily went through the tyres. You made sure you carried a puncture-mending outfit and knew how to use it.

Our village stonebreaker was a very cheery man, much liked by adults and children. Everyone gave him a greeting or stopped for a little chat. I asked him once if he liked sitting all day stonebreaking, which I thought must be a very dull job, but to my surprise he said, 'Bless you missie, I enjoys it. I has all you children coming by with your little chats, and I has a cheery word with everyone else who goes by. I get the exercise walking to work and home again and doing me garden of an evening. If I worked in the fields or on a farm it's likely I wouldn't see a soul all day.'

Another man we children liked was the man who drove the steamroller. He was a big, red-faced man and was also fond of children. The steamroller had a lovely brass horse on the front with 'Invicta' in brass letters below it. The horse was prancing on its hind legs and I was more attracted by that horse than by the engine. Engine drivers in those days took a great pride in their engines and that driver was no exception. All the brasswork was highly polished and the paintwork gleamed as if it had just left the works. The driver himself was usually as black as a tinker. I used to worry him for a ride on the roller and he used to say, 'No, my gal, I can't do that, it's too black up here. What on earth would your mother say if you went home with your pretty dress and nice pinny as black as I am. I reckon she'd give me what for and no mistake. I'll tell you what I'll do instead – you can have a duster and polish the little horse. Mind you, you must promise never to go in front of the roller when it's moving, because I can't see you and if you fell in front and got hurt I would never forgive myself and your mother would never forgive me. So you can see your little horse all you like when we are standing still.'

In the 1920s things were very grim for most people and many farmers lost everything they had. Those like my grandfather who was also a dealer survived because they had another string to their bow and were not entirely dependent on the farm.

Once grandfather was trying to sell a beast to a butcher; it was a young two-year-old in really prime condition. My grandfather asked the butcher £16 for it. I was weeding in the garden and heard all that went on through the hedge. Mr Stevens the butcher offered £14 but Grandpa would not take it. I was highly amused to hear Grandfather say, 'Well Master Stevens, I don't know whether you're a fool or whether I are, but one of us is and it aint me.'

During the First World War farm wages went up to £2 10s. but in the depression of the 1920s they were cut by half to 25s. I often helped out on other farms at haytime and harvest. The casual labour rate for men was 1s. an hour and for women it was 6d. an hour. As I was very experienced in all farm work and could do most jobs as well as a man and certainly better than most casual workers, I refused to work for 6d. an hour and said if I was doing a man's work I expected a man's pay, and I got it too. The men also got a beer allowance, which the farmer brought to the field, sometimes in a small barrel and sometimes in bottles. As I was teetotal I got 3s. 6d. a week in lieu of the beer.

For years I worked for a Mr Moon who did contract work for

Ada Cousins, a friend of Mrs Tibbetts, at work at a dairy near Watford, c. 1926

people. I used to cycle to his yard, then all of us working for him would ride to work in the big farm wagon. I did all the jobs from turning the hay to rick building, but I liked working with horses best. As I was experienced, they put me on the great wagons to load the hay, which had to be done very carefully to keep it upright or it would slip off the wagon.

There were no balers then, all the hay was loose. When it was dry it was raked into rows. When I was small that was done with wooden rakes, but by 1914 they had wide rakes with iron tines, pulled by a horse. As one person raked, several people with forks put the hay into heaps, that we called cocks. That was another job

21

that had to be done carefully, so that if it rained the water would run down the heap and not soak into it and ruin the hay. When the hay was ready to load, the wagon went along between the rows and two men pitched those heaps onto the wagon, one on each side. That was another very skilled job. A good pitcher would pick up each heap very cleanly and put it just where you wanted it, without disturbing the hay. He would make sure the hay was the right way round so that it slipped easily out and the heap stayed put – an art I learnt from my father. If it was done properly you could see each heap when you went to unload the wagon, and when you lifted them with your fork they came up in one neat pile. That made unloading much easier. Today those old skills are not often needed as all the work is done by tractors and balers.

There are still a few farmers who farm in the old way with horses; there is one near here. Some farms and estates still make hay and harvest oats in the old way to cater for the racing stables and hunt stables, who like sweet, clean hay and oats and also straw for their valuable horses. Hay made by machine is often a bit damp when baled, and dusty as well. It is not used for horses as it causes bad wind and respiratory problems. With tractors and machinery there is always dust and that gets baled with the hay.

When I was young, the best straw was saved for thatching and straw plaiting. The plait for straw boaters (hats) was made with whole straw, but the straw for ladies' hats was split into four or five pieces. This was done on a simple device consisting of a piece of wood, well planed, which had three holes bored in it. Wires or wheels were fitted in each hole and the straw was split to the size required for whatever type of hat it was to be used for. Straw boaters were made from the whole straw with the straw points cut out and only four straws were used at one time. I often saw my Gran making them when I was small. She often tried to teach me, but it was a difficult plait pattern and I never mastered it. I did learn several other patterns which I can still do, and I still make them into hats.

Women also did beadwork and sewing buttons on shirts and trousers for so much a thousand buttons. They sewed leather straps on braces, for which they got 1s. 6d. per dozen pairs of braces. There were six straps on each pair; it was slave labour! That went on until the early 1930s. I can remember helping my mother doing beadwork, which was sewing beads on evening dresses. The material was stamped with a dot for each bead. It was a tedious job and more than poorly paid. I liked fruit picking or farm work much better.

CHAPTER TWO

HAY TRUSSING

Mrs Lilian Till gives an illustrated account of working with her father, a haytrusser, in Wiltshire.

My parents were Mr and Mrs George Hopkins and we came to Wootton Bassett in 1912. My father was a hay dealer and cutter and came to Wiltshire, a good agricultural area. As a very little girl I recall living in the country, often miles from a town. There was no electricity in those days, only oil lamps and candles. Our house was often isolated and very lonely. The lavatory was situated at the bottom of a long garden – there were two toilets, one for grown-ups and one for children, which I understand now were dirt closets.

My mother worked very hard looking after us all, as she had seven children and life was not easy for her in those days. She did her washing in a scullery where the copper was in a corner. I remember it had a big wooden lid that mother used to dish the clothes on to. A well in the garden was the only means of water so it was hard work for her drawing the water for washing. The copper was heated by a fire underneath which had to be kept stoked up to keep the clothes boiling.

My mother was a wonderful cook and as we kept pigs we always had one killed and brought it indoors for food. Mother would cure it and there was always plenty of bacon, hams, hocks of bacon and lovely backbones which she made into delicious stews. She would

Hay Trussing

My father used a very big knife to cut out the 'trusses' which had to weigh about half a hundredweight each. This was a skilful job. The trusses were carried down the rick and put into a 'hay press' where strings were attached and after levering the press, little trusses were produced.

Mr Till holding his hay knife

Cutting the rick

Carrying down the trusses

also clean the intestines and make chitterling, lots of home-made lard and home-made faggots.

We always had a garden and my mother produced many vegetables and fruit. We were very self-supporting and going to the town was a treat to look forward to, and that was either by walking or pony and trap.

We had many miles to walk to school and I believe our parents had to pay for us to go. Looking back now I can remember playing hoops and spinning our tops in the road. No motor cars to worry us but the roads were not like they are today, smooth and easy. The road-menders would sit on top of a pile of big stones put there by the council and hammer and bash away at them all day, smashing them into smaller pieces, ready for the steamroller to come along and roll them into the road. We didn't like this because we couldn't spin our tops.

When we came to Wootton Bassett my father was working for a hay firm that had secured the Army contracts to supply hay for the horses. This took him to Salisbury Plain so it was decided that mother and two or three of us children went with him. So off we set in pony and trap which seemed a very long journey. This was my first taste of camping. Father provided us with a lovely big tent made of tarpaulin and a bed made of trusses of hay to sleep on. How well I remember running through the grass in the early morning dew and paddling in a sheep trough that mother had scrubbed out. The skylarks seemed to sing all day, soaring in the sky until out of sight. What happy days!

I can remember some of the first motor cars and aeroplanes and also seeing a Zeppelin. It was a hard life during the First World War and so were the conditions that followed – unemployment and the General Strike in 1926. Some people I knew were affected by the Means Test and practically their whole homes were taken away from them.

I started work at the age of fourteen and earned 6s. a week for many long hours. During this time it was a struggle as money was

Using the hay press

Piling up the trusses

28

hard to come by, so my parents decided to breed Aylesbury ducks. Eventually we killed, plucked and dressed them and sent them to Leadenhall Market in London. We also bred turkeys for Christmas. Two of my sisters, my younger brother and myself joined the Young Farmers Pig Club and reared our own pigs until they were suitable for bacon and then they were taken away to be killed. This all happened in the 1920s.

In 1937, I married a railway locomotive engineer. Our wages were very low, earning £1. 10s 0d. one week and £3. 0s. 0d. the next, and paying for our house at £3. 5s. 0d. per month was a big strain on our income. Of course, the price of houses was very different from today as ours was £1,000, which took us twenty-one years to pay. These were depressing years and then came the Second World War.

CHAPTER THREE

RURAL CHURCHES IN YORKSHIRE

Mrs Jean Mook from Yorkshire describes the importance of religion in the life of the villages.

During the 1930s, when I was a pupil at the local village school, religion played a significant part in the lives of schoolchildren. I attended a Church of England School and every week, without fail, the vicar from the next parish came to address all the children. There was no church in our village. There was a Methodist Chapel. Living on a very isolated farm, my younger sister and I went to Chapel Sunday school every Sunday morning, having to walk $1^{1}/_{2}$ miles in each direction. At Sunday school we sang hymns and the teacher read stories from the Bible to us. There were two very important events in the calendar of the Methodist Sunday school; one was the Sunday School Anniversary and the second was the Sunday School Outing which was always to Scarborough, which would be about 40 miles away.

For the Sunday School Anniversary every child had to memorize a poem, either with a religious theme or a well-known poem by authors such as Kipling, Tennyson or Wordsworth. Those children who sang well had to sing a solo or perhaps a duet. There were two performances of this: the first on the Sunday afternoon and the second on either the Monday or Tuesday evening. Most of the children got a new outfit of clothes for the anniversary and after that occasion it was worn only for special events. The chapel was always well attended for this event, and the Sunday school teachers certainly put a lot of hard work into preparing this event.

The most looked-forward to event in the whole year was the Sunday School Outing to Scarborough. We went by coach and during the previous winter the adults in the village had been raising money by having whist drives to finance this treat. I can remember being too excited to sleep the night before. We had to walk to the bus departure point. On getting onto the coach we were given 6d. and a four ounce bag of sweets. On arriving at Scarborough we immediately made for the beach with our buckets and spades, our mothers carrying our bathing costumes and towels. At lunch-time we all met at a café where a meal of fish and chips had been ordered. If funds permitted we were each given a stick of rock to eat on the way home. It never seemed to rain on these occasions although I can't think that we were always lucky with the weather.

Apart from a few days when I was about five years old, this was the only time that I went to the seaside. This outing was only available to regular attenders at Sunday school. My mother had been brought up in a strict Church of England home which was insistent on going to be 'churched' after the births of my brother and youngest sister, even though it meant cycling three-and-a-half miles to the nearest church.

Christmas meant carol singing. Choirs from both church and chapel walked miles to outlying farmhouses to sing carols and usually they were invited inside to partake of Christmas cake and a drink of anything they fancied. The ladies normally opted for tea, but the men always asked for something stronger, whisky or port wine being favourites. Carol singing was a social activity which was very much looked forward to.

Another highlight of the church year was the annual Harvest Festival or 'Harvest Home' as it was usually referred to by the older people. On that occasion much greater congregations could be expected at all the services, i.e. on Sunday afternoon, Sunday evening, and Monday or Tuesday evening. As you will no doubt know, the Methodist Church depends a lot on lay preachers, and at the Harvest Festival a prominent farmer or someone connected with farming would usually conduct all the services. Concluding the worship on the weekday evening, supper would be available for those who wanted it. The venue was the schoolroom attached to all chapels and the food was provided by the women who were regular chapelgoers. This invariably consisted of ham, egg or cheese sand-wiches, sausage rolls and homemade pastries and cakes. A collection would be taken and the proceeds sometimes went to the chapel itself or to a Methodist Missionary charity.

Another custom in the Methodist Church was the invitation to tea to the preacher into the homes of chapel stewards and regular attenders on Sunday when the two services were Sunday afternoon and evening. My late mother-in-law always felt very honoured when the preacher, who sometimes could be the minister in charge of the Circuit, accepted her invitation to have tea with her family. The usual menu was cold boiled ham, tomatoes, trifle and a selec-tion of home-made cakes and pastries. Now most chapels have just one service on Sunday mornings and only a few have two services every Sunday, the second service being in the evening, so this cus-tom is dying out.

Although Easter and Whitsuntide are important festivals in the Christian Church, as far as I can remember not much importance was attached to either of them. At Easter most of the women would be spring-cleaning, an annual ritual most strictly adhered to, and the farmers and the agricultural workers who made up most of the population of the villages would be busy preparing the land for the sowing of the crops. At that time 90 per cent of the corn was sown in spring; now most of the corn is drilled in autumn.

I think it is fair to conclude that religion played a significant part in the lives of people who lived in rural England, there being few other diversions. I think that what applied to Methodists in the 1930s would also apply to members of the Church of England, but I have no knowledge of what Roman Catholics did. I am sure that more people attended church or chapel during the 1930s than they do now. At the village church where I now live the congregations are very small, usually under ten. I am a regular worshipper at the Methodist Chapel at the next village and there they have two services each Sunday.

CHAPTER FOUR

FRUIT FARMING IN KENT

Mrs Ruth Brockwell gives a detailed account of both women's domestic work in a farmhouse and their work in the fields and orchards on a fruit farm.

I was born on 5 March 1924 at Queen Mary's Hospital, London. My mother was a schoolteacher and my father had been a pupil on a farm for several years to learn all aspects of farming, specializing in fruit farming. Shortly after I was born he became a farm manager.

When I was five years old we moved from Essex after my father had finished his training and came to Parkgate Farm, Tenterden, Kent, where he was to take up his post as a farm manager. The farm had a very large house: one half of it was the original old farmhouse which would be about three or four hundred years old, and the other half had been added in the Regency period – a very tall, imposing-looking part. It stood on a hill with a most beautiful view right across Romney Marshes to the coast at Hastings. It really was very beautiful round that way; the woods and the fields and all the apple orchards really looked lovely.

The house was typical of the farmhouses in those days. In the kitchen there was a big brick copper, which later, of course, came out and a black stove that had to be blackleaded. I always remember my mother blackleading the stove – quite a regular job to do and very hard work too. The kitchen had beautiful beams – one heavy beam right across the centre but beautiful beams all in the walls and

34

across the ceiling – and a very uneven brick floor made of ordinary bricks, not tiles. An ordinary redbrick floor was an awful job to keep clean because of all the dust that got between the bricks. The bathroom was very sparse, just an ordinary bath and a toilet with no fittings, and we had a well outside in a shed – it was always called the pump shed. The old pump was a tall upright thing; you pumped the handle up and down. There was a little hatch at the back that you could lift up and see down the well. You always had to be very careful that you didn't tread on it in case it ever gave way. At that time we didn't have water laid on in the house; we relied on that well and a spring that we found down the farm. When we had baths it was quite a chore because the water had to be pumped up and heated in the copper and carried by bucket to fill up the bath. The bathrooms were so cold – it was not a very enjoyable experience.

In the kitchen there was a big open chimney corner where we had big log fires – there was no electricity. We had Aladdin lamps all around the house and you took a candle to see your way to bed. If you sat round the fireplace it was lovely – a glowing warmth. In fact, sometimes it was too hot but if you sat the other side of the room which was very big you would freeze, so the method of heating was not all that good. A lot of the heat went up the chimney which was massive. There was one large chimney in the middle of the house, the sort you see in a lot of these farmhouses. The wooden floors were all solid oak. We had a staircase which curved round and another staircase that curved up to two attics, and they were all solid oak which we used to clean with beeswax. It was all very hard work. You would sweep all the matting and you had to wait for the dust to settle, then you would start dusting and when you finished the room would look beautiful but an hour later the dust would start to come back again. It was a far cry from cleaning these days when if you clean a room at least it stays clean for a while. But cleaning the kitchen with all those beams, that was where you used to get the dust. We had not been there very long before the copper was pulled out and that made more room. The old cooker went and we had a lovely Aga cooker, which was really a great improvement and it made the kitchen look a lot nicer too, and the bathrooms were fitted out better. The whole house gradually was improved without spoiling the character of it.

My mother worked like mad. There were fourteen rooms in the house and I hardly ever remember seeing her sitting down relaxing. I was brought up to help her with a lot of the chores because in those days when you were little you just had to learn to run the house. She used to do all her own cooking, breadmaking, cakes, everything; you never bought anything, it was all home-made. We had a big pantry; you could walk into it and round it and the shelves from floor to ceiling were lined with home-made jams, marmalade, jellies, lemon curd, fruit bottling, everything that you would need, and the flavour of everything was really lovely. We made our own butter: the milk used to be poured into big pans and left to settle and it was my job to skim the cream off the top and put it into a big basin. Then the buttermilk was used either to make cream cheeses or it was fed back to the animals. The pigs often used to have the buttermilk but everything was made use of. I used to make the cottage cheese, put it in the muslin and leave it to strain. We used to have to help to make the butter and then when I was a little bit older I used to deliver it to all the people in the neighbourhood.

My mother worked very hard indeed and in the summer months she would go out on the farm and pick the fruit. The strawberries would come in and she would pack them and sell some of them at the door. Really life was all work. There was very little leisure – there wasn't time for it. I think my father was always working. Occasionally he would have an evening free.

My mother had a routine of work. She would get up and there was breakfast. It would be a full cooked breakfast: bacon, eggs, sausage, or it would be scrambled eggs on toast or poached eggs; sometimes it would be kippers, followed by toast and marmalade and your cup of tea. Then she would clear away and wash up all the breakfast things. After washing up it was make the beds – they had to be made by a certain time. They were big beds, with thick feather mattresses which you had to hump about and turn, with loads of blankets. She used to turn the bed over, hump it up, put all these blankets on and tuck the bed up. It wasn't like turning a duvet over. At night it was so cold but you always had all the windows wide open in the bedroom. It just was not considered healthy to sleep with your windows closed or even with one little window open. It was freezing but everyone seemed very healthy.

After the beds were all made it was what she termed as 'lamps and fireplaces'. All the lamps were brought into the kitchen, the wicks trimmed, the glasses cleaned and filled with paraffin. The candles were replaced and the candlesticks which were brass were polished. And then all the fireplaces had to be cleaned out, the fires laid and the Aga cooker riddled out, and all of this was done in remarkably quick time. When those jobs were done there was washing and cleaning and then they would all stop for morning coffee and buns. My father always came in from the farm for this. Anyone who visited our house in the morning was always asked into the kitchen and they had coffee and buns. We knew when the baker was going to get there, when the grocer was going to get there, and the butcher. All of them used to come and have their coffee and buns and it always seemed strange that my mother, doing all that work, gearing for a 12 o'clock dinner, had time to sit and have that break. Once that break was over she would start cooking the dinner. It was a big dinner – there was lots of cooking to be done for it. After dinner there was the washing up and the clearing up and, of course, she would do whatever she had to do, whether it was her afternoon for baking or her afternoon for ironing.

Everything was done to a routine. Every year, January she called her month of repair: she spent January doing all the mending and patching of the household linen. When the sheets were thin they were turned about with a seam put very finely down the centre to get the wear from the edges – they were 'turned about' and all the little tiny holes were darned very fine. My grandmother taught me how to darn. In the summer the months were taken up with jam-making, bottling and all that sort of thing and then, of course, at the beginning of November, she would start all the Christmas cooking because it was all done well in advance.

Dinner was always at 12 o'clock and 1 o'clock on Sundays because there were no workmen about then. Our dinners always started off with a good home-made soup, unless, of course, the weather was hot – in the summer it was different. We had roast twice a week: Sundays and Thursdays. Mondays was always cold meat and something simple like a potato cheese or cauliflower cheese, jacket potatoes, or something like that because Monday was taken up with wash-day. There would be toad-in-the-hole, sausages, lovely stew made with oxtails or with steak or lamb, meat puddings, meat pies – all plain, simple foods but very nourishing and very good. There was always a nice pudding afterwards. Steam puddings, fruit pies, queen of puddings, mainly got from Helen Burke, the well-known cookery expert of the day, or Mrs Beeton or the old Radiation book of the day, as we used to call it, or *Good Housekeeping*. They were all very substantial meals – it was the real old English food.

We used to have what we called a high tea which was fish or eggs, or it could be cold meat with salad. Another night, especially Sundays, we would have home-made scones, jam and cream, and home-made bread and butter, cheeses and lots of cakes. There was always a jolly good variety of cakes but the seed cake was a favourite. There were also a lot of iced cakes – iced sponges, iced cherry cakes – and it wasn't just a little icing, it was thick icing.

They were our main meals of the day. Everything was home-made which made the meals very nourishing and the flavour very good too. My father kept bees on the farm for the pollination of the fruit in the orchards, so we used to have lovely honey. You used to get the honeycombs and the real local honey. We were a fruit farm so all the fruit was picked straight off the farm and there really is nothing like it. We used to do all this fruit bottling and also my mother used to salt down runner beans. We didn't have freezers then so the runner beans were sliced and salted in big earthenware crocks. Eggs were pickled in big crocks.

When they used to kill a pig, my father would make beautiful brawn and home-made sausages and we used to have our own bacon that was home-smoked. You wouldn't get anything like it now. I doubt if you would get anything with that flavour. He would go out shooting and bring rabbits in and they would hang up in our cellar. We would have rabbit for dinner and pheasants, pigeons and partridges. When I was quite a little girl I used to cook all these type of things for dinner because I had to learn how to do it. We used to do jugged pigeons. You put several of these pigeons in one of the earthenware crocks and put flavouring and liquid and a bit of onion in and then we used to put it in the slow oven of the Aga. The Aga has two ovens: one is a fast ordinary cooking oven and the other is what is termed as a slow oven and we would put the pigeon in over night and the next day it was cooked just beautiful and the gravy was lovely. The pheasants and the partridges were done like a roast dinner. The rabbits were made into pies or casseroles with a piece of nice streaky pork with them. When we had a goose for our dinner, the fat was all poured off and left to get cold and solid and then it was rubbed into all the farm boots to make them waterproof, and that was a jolly good waterproofing too.

We had a brook going through the garden and my father did a little fishing. There were a lot of eels in it and he often used to catch these eels. I used to go fishing with him and watch him but I didn't like to see him catch eels – they wriggled about too much. We used to cook them like ordinary fish: fry them or he used to souse them in a parsley sauce and that was another very tasty meal. There were so many different varieties of food you could get just from the farm and it was all fresh, nicely cooked and wholesome and there were no additives to it. I cannot explain the difference in the flavour but they were really lovely. It was a lot of work preparing the meals. There was a lot of work in everything because there were no food mixers or processors, or dishwashers to clear up afterwards. You just beat everything up by hand and some of it jolly well took some beating too and it all had to be cooked for longer than what the cookers take now. You had lots of washing up to do and you hadn't got all the amount of hot water you have now because it was about four or five years before we had water laid on from the mains. We were there eight or nine years before we had electricity and there never was gas up there. The main drainage was put in later on and that came in after the water so we gradually did get modernized. I don't think we ever really took any notice of it. You just went to bed at night with a hot-water bottle and candle-light, into a freezing cold room and you got lovely and warm once you had got into bed. It was just getting up to a freezing cold room in the morning that was the trouble, but I think we accepted it in those days.

We had this big copper when we moved in but it was taken out after a while because it was so cumbersome. My mother did all the washing and she had one of those huge wooden mangles. There was a bath put underneath and she turned the handle and I used to have to lift the washing up out of the bath and put it through the rollers. She would turn the handle and push the washing through and get all the water out of it; that was what you might call an old-fashioned idea of a spin-drier but it took the worst of the wet out. Then you pegged the washing out in the clean, fresh air where it dried up beautifully white and all the things that needed starching were starched – everything was done so carefully. When the washing was dry I used to help my mother to fold the sheets and all the big items and we would get them in the mangle again. I would have to pull them out tight while she turned the handle and you used to do as good a job on them as ironing. For the sheets and things you used to just fold them up and they were finished. It was a very simple way of doing things but, of course, it was not as nice as what you get now I suppose, yet they always looked nice and lasted a lot longer. But there was such a lot of work in washing and ironing. When we were ironing – naturally there were no electric irons in those days – all we had was the black irons that were put on the stove to heat. When they were hot you just spat on them and made sure they were hot enough to do your ironing. You did all the linens and things that needed a very hot iron first and when the iron was cooling down you did the things that needed a cooler iron. You would then get the second iron and start over again. Ironing all had to be done in a certain rotation and so you had a pile of things that needed a hot iron and a pile of things that need-ed a cooler iron, and you would rotate from one to the other. The ironing then was much more difficult than just having an electric iron to plug in, switch on, hey hoe! There you are!

Later on when we had even more work to do with the farm, the stockman's wife that lived in one of the farm buildings did my mother's washing. I remember she used to come up Monday mornings and get a great big linen basket piled up with dirty wash-ing, all the bed linen and everything and she would take it down to her house and do all the washing. It would come back to us ironed and ready for use and we paid her 5s. for doing that. The amount of washing she did and the work that was put into it and yet they thought it was well paid in those days.

We had a grocer in Tenterden that we went to and there was a man who used to cycle up to the house twice a week. He would go to all the houses of people that dealt with that shop. I think it was Tuesdays and Thursdays and my mother would have an order written out of the groceries that she wanted. So he would come in and sit down and she would make him the usual coffee or tea or whatever he wanted and give him the grocery list. He was a very quiet man; he worked there for years and he always just plodded up the road on his bicycle at the same pace, never hurrying. He would sit down and quietly read through the list but he would never just take it that that was all because not only did they want the trade but they wanted to make sure you hadn't forgotten anything. He would say to my mother, 'Is that everything Mrs Page? Are you sure you have got everything down? Nothing else you can think of? Let me think now.' Then he would sit down in the chair, and as if it was imprinted on his memory from doing it so many times, he would recite this whole list of things in the shop that they sold to see if it jogged her memory of anything that she wanted. How he remembered everything I'll never know but even after all these years I can remember part of that recital. The things I can remember were: soap, soda, starch, blues, blacking, black lead, biscuits of any kind, and that was where the question mark was, then a little pause, and then he would go on to the next bit of this long list. I thought this was rather a good little rhyme and it has stuck in my mind all these years. The next day the groceries would be delivered, all in a box and put in the kitchen ready for mother to put away. Then that caller would have a cup of tea or coffee and so life went on.

The farm consisted of 164 acres of pasture and arable land. It was in the village of Tenterden but the land spread into the parishes of Broadenden, Benenden and Biddenden. Therefore we had four tithes to pay because we spread into the four parishes. We employed eight men permanently and in the winter we used to have two women who came in nearly all the time, unless the weather was very bad, to help with the work on the fruit trees – pruning and that sort of thing. We had a group of women from Tenterden who used to come in all through the summer for fruit picking and packing and they used to come in year after year. It was always the same women and later on their children as they grew up sometimes used to come up. At first it was only one or two but when we got more orchards going we needed more people. My father managed the farm and one of the men was a stockman and he had an assistant. The stockman was a proper old character; he had lived in the area all his life and had been on farms and always worked with animals. His name was William but he was always known as Bogey; all the villagers around knew Bogey and he had a son who was also William and he was called Buns. I don't know why they were called this. I think there were lots of people nick-named like that. The other three men were all young lads that had come from school and they stayed with us for years. One of them very sadly died during the war. He was called up for active service because we were only allowed so many people to stay on the farm and he was the one over. He died in Malta, but the others stayed with us until the farm was eventually sold when my parents died.

When we moved in, it was pasture and arable but it was intended to become a fruit farm with some cattle as well, so the orchards were planted. I remember them planting the orchards: such tiny lit-tle trees they looked but they grew. It ended up that we had 37 acres of apple orchards but there were 33 acres of woodland and the rest was pasture and arable. The woods were lovely. The farm was a very pretty farm. It had parts of it that were like little beauty spots of their own and you could go to them and sit there and think. Where could you go to find anything more beautiful than this? There was this lovely brook that ran right through the woods and they found the remains of a Roman road going down leading to the brook. A lot of the names of the woods – there was Bright Wood and Barnshawe Wood – were all related to Roman things or something to do with history. It was very pretty and when the orchards grew and you had the blossom forming on the trees in the spring, it really was beautiful.

Our hayfields were a mass of buttercups, clover and daisies. I used to go and sit at the edges of the hayfield and look across and it was just like a sea of grass and thick wild flowers. I don't think there are anywhere near as many wild flowers about now, which I am sure is probably due to all these chemicals they put on the land. This was brought home to me when I went to the Isle of Arran recently and I saw an abundance of wild flowers there. They haven't used a lot of chemicals although I believe they do now because they have started spraying the fir forests that they have put up.

There were various sheds in the back yard, but it wasn't really a yard, just a vast area of green at the back of the house. Lower down we had pigsties and there was a large oast house. There hadn't been hops on that farm for a very long time and the oast house was never used for hop drying while we were there. Other farmers around us grew hops and I used to go down and sometimes help them with the hop picking. I saw the hop drying which was another interesting thing but our oast house was used more as a storage unit. Lower down the drive we had the cowsheds and lovely big old barns where we kept the animal feed and different things including hay. They were really old low-roofed barns and there were the stables and an open-ended shed where all the farm implements were put. We had a big Dutch barn built and later on we had a big cold storage built for the apples. When we first went there the farmyard was very primitive. It was more of a poor man's farm I suppose, as the barns were in need of repair and there was a lot of old equipment.

There was a tennis court on the other side of the drive; when there had been wealthier people in the farmhouse, it had been used for the young ladies to play tennis but we never used it for tennis. We used it to keep geese and chickens on. We got very modern buildings which blended in very well with the others. The old buildings were still there but they had been done up and improved so that they would last for years; they still looked lovely and kept their original character. My father was very particular about how the outbuildings were kept and the roads, tracks and drives which led down to the farm buildings and the ponds, with a view in mind to the cattle having reasonably clean areas to walk through instead of mud. We would go to some of the farms near us where a farmer didn't look after his farm and farmyard and barns, and when they were bringing in the cows for milking, they would be walking through filth right up their legs. My father would never allow it and used to keep everything clean and in good condition. He used to say if you saw a farmyard was well looked after, you knew you had a good farmer but if a farmyard was very mucky and not tended to then you had a lazy farmer.

We had three horses when we first went to the farm – two mares and one stallion. The two mares were used as a team for ploughing and all that type of work. We had some young foals and as they got bigger they were used or we sold them. I remember Dad going behind with the plough. We had tractors later on but when they were doing it by hand they always used to take a great pride in the ploughing. I remember him always saying you must keep a straight line down the field and a good turn on the headland and I have often heard him remarking when he has been looking at the ploughing, if some of the other men had done it, that they hadn't done a very good turn, or if he was looking at other farms where they had ploughed their fields, I have heard him remark, 'Well, he hasn't made a very good job of the headland.' So it must have been quite an important thing that the rows were straight and the headland was neat and you had a nice edging all round your field.

We had a lot of pigs and a lovely herd of bullocks, and about a dozen cows – enough to give us the milk that we needed and we used to let people around buy milk from us. We had one bull and a lot of sheep. The bullocks we did go in for in a very big way. They were beautiful animals. That was when we had an extra barn built with all the pens in it for when we brought them in for winter.

I remember the first time I heard my father say they were getting a tractor. We had these lovely horses but there was so much work to do it was much quicker to have this tractor. It was a caterpillar tractor and they started using that for all the work and the horses were not needed so much and eventually another tractor turned up, and that was a Fordson. We ended up having three tractors and by then, of course, the horses were older and they needed retiring so they all went to a rest home. I thought it was very sad because horses are a lovely part of farm life. The tractors that we had then were very different to the ones you see about now. It was a basic tractor that was used solely for pulling whatever implement was needed, so it was doing nothing but replacing the horse. But nowadays all of the tractors are being geared up to do all of the work.

Haymaking was a very busy time in the summer because the farmers were watching how well the fields were coming along and how rich the hay looked, and as soon as it was time, and the weather was good, everyone got ready for cutting the hay in case the weather turned again. At first, it was the horses that were doing the work and the hay was turned by hand by the men. They used to go out and cut the hay with the horses pulling the gear to do it and then when the sun shone on it the men would go with pitchforks and turn all round the edges. But the horses pulled the hay rakes. They went all over the field but round the edges, where they didn't do a very good job, so men would go and turn it with pitchforks. Then there was getting all the hay up and bringing it in and making up the haystacks. It is very clever how they are made. The men used to start at seven in the morning and work until it got dark at night. It was very hot but there was a very good spirit among the men and they all worked in together. My father used to go out haymaking; he was not one of those farm managers who sat in an office all day. He went out with the men and he probably worked harder than any of them and did all the things they did. In the mid-morning and mid-afternoon mother used to make a big pot of tea. We had a huge 'Auld Lang Syne' china teapot and we had a wicker linen basket and all these white cups, that were kept solely for haymaking, harvesting, and fruit picking, were put into it. And the tea was made in this great big pot, milk was included, and if I wasn't at school I would help mother. If I was at school someone else would help carry this basket out to the haymakers with the tea, milk and sugar. There were always loads of buns for them to have a tuck in. She would go out to the field wherever they were working and put this lot down.

If they were working too far away, some of the men would just come up and get it but not often because they were too busy getting on with the job. They would usually sit down for ten minutes and have this drink and then back the basket would come and all the cups, etc. would have to be washed up – and that was all in the middle of a morning's work. And mid-afternoon about 3 o'clock out she would go again, and they would have another lot of drinks. When they finished at night, if it was very late and they had had a busy day, my Dad used to have them all up to the house and then there would be a drink of beer or cider or whatever they wanted and they would have that before they went home. There was always a very good spirit among them. I think there was more of a community spirit then. I suppose it was just one of the annual events but it was very satisfying to see all the hay brought up, all the stacks made and the job finished. There was always a great sigh of relief all round if the weather held up and we got it in while it was dry.

Then there was the harvesting; that was another very busy time. They used to go along and cut the corn, and put it up in stooks all the way down the field. Then the workers would go round and if the weather was extremely hot, and it dried and ripened it through pretty well, that was all right, but if it was wet they would go round and turn the stooks to get them so that the wet side was dried out. Then, of course, they used to cart them all in and put them into stacks.

Later on the threshing engine would come round. There would be a man that did this threshing with a group of men and he would come along with a threshing engine and usually a caravan on the back that either he or the men lived in. There were some near us that took their families with them as well when they went round to do the threshing. They would usually stay approximately two or three days to do all the threshing. Now we have combine harvesters, but then you were cutting the corn, putting it up in stooks, getting it dried, then loading it up onto wagons and bringing it in. First of all it was wagons with horses, in later years wagons with tractors, bringing it into the farmyard and all the time and trouble making the stacks. Then when it was the threshing time, that was another job that started early in the morning and they worked through until dark. It was a filthy job. The men were absolutely black when they had finished. My Dad always had his dogs all around him and all the little cats from the farmyard would appear from everywhere – we had a lot of cats running wild around the farmyard to keep the mice down. As they were getting to the bottom of the stack the mice used to run out of it and the dogs and cats were all flying everywhere catching them. It was quite an experience, all these little creatures going everywhere. The threshing was a long, dirty, noisy job. When that was all finished with, that was another end of season. You realized then that the autumn was upon you. When they were doing this harvesting, the old teapot came out even more frequently because they needed some refreshment. It was very thirsty work and we kept going several times a day with tea and a snack and the beer and the cider. It was a good time all round I think; people seemed to enjoy it. So that is another time that is lost these days because combine harvesters have got nowhere near that atmosphere.

A job that was always done in the winter was the drainage of the ditches. It was quite important; a lot of the fields needed drainage. There was a drainage system with pipes put in running through into ditches and every winter the ditches were cleaned out and cut away. It was quite a performance clearing all the ditches surrounding certain fields. Some fields were more important than others and we made sure their ditches were clear and there were no blocked drains so that when we had heavy rain and the water gathered, we didn't have any flooding. Another thing was the hedges; all the hedges round the fields were cut regularly every year and kept to a nice height and tended well. The verges along the road were all cut back and cleared so that there was no high growth of weeds and it all looked neat and tidy and left an open aspect all around the field.

We used to have trees along certain places where we needed a wind-break. Hedges were there for a purpose; they were there to act as a wind-break, to shelter things from the high winds and also as a boundary line to keep cattle out. The gates all had to have a periodic overhaul to make sure they had all got latches on them. Some farmers didn't bother; you would go to a farm and find broken down gates, ditches overflowing, hedges all unruly and it made such a big difference to the appearance of the farm and also to the running of it.

When I was small, it was quite common to see the charcoal burners in the woods. There were several clearings in the woods round near us – not on our farm, but on adjoining places where there was woodland – where there were charcoal burners. I don't think you see a lot of that now either, but it was fascinating to watch.

Later on we had fruit. You would start in the winter and the first major thing would be pruning the fruit trees. My father and one or two of the other men that were specialized in that sort of work would prune the trees. There is a great art in that because if you do not prune a tree properly, you don't get the right shaped tree and then you don't get good fruit. I remember him saying you leave the centres open for the sun to get through and you shape the tree well. And they used to prune all the trees; all the wood would drop to the ground and then the women that we employed would come along and pick up all the pruning. They would wear a big apron around the waist, over their coats. They would put this big apron thing on, then they would haul it up and put all their prunings in it. They had a scoop thing to put them in and then when it was full up, they would go over and tip it into a big heap. When they had a big enough heap they would light it and they would then have bonfires going all day. It was wintertime so it was a very cold job going round pruning and picking up all the prunings. Then they would rake all around to keep the ground clear and they would light the bonfire. We often used to put the potatoes in there so we had jacket potatoes when it was lunch-time – a nice warming thought after a cold job. Then there would be the spraying. I cannot remember how many times they sprayed the trees in the winter but there was nowhere near as much spraying done then as there is now.

When the blossom came on the trees, we used to go round the trees blossom thinning. This was the job the women did and I did later on when I worked on the farm. If you had a group of three blossoms you would knock out two and leave one, so that whereas you would originally have had three apples, by knocking out those two little buds, you would get one good-sized apple. Otherwise you would have three tiny little apples that probably would come to nothing much and they wouldn't have a very good flavour. When you think of it we used to go round every tree in those orchards and knock all the blossoms off. It was a tedious job but it was done and it did improve the fruit. Later on they changed over to what they must have found was a better method; they waited until the fruit had just formed and when the blossoms had gone and there was a little tiny fruit there, they would knock off two fruits and leave one so that all over the tree there were 'groups of one' instead of groups of two or three, and then we used to end up with a really first class crop of fruit. We used to enter the fruit into the local show. They were very big fruit shows and we used to get lots of prizes for it but I think it was only because a lot of care was taken in growing it. We used to do this blossom thinning and then later the apple thinning. By then it would be springtime.

In the meantime, other things were going on. The sheep and cattle were being attended to and in the spring you got the lambing season. The corn was planted – this was done during the winter – and then when the lambing was over and the weather got warmer, there was the sheep shearing. That used to be done by the stock-man on the farm. He used to do all the sheep and then they were dipped because otherwise they would get the fly. I have seen sheep with the sheep fly and it is an awful thing to get because the sheep is in a lot of pain. Dipping the sheep did prevent it.

Strawberry picking would be the next thing. We used to grow strawberries and we had beautiful fruit and again that was very well looked after. When I think back now I cannot believe what we used to do. We got all the old potatoes that weren't any good for eating – the old ones that came out of the clamps that were not much good. I forgot to say we used to grow potatoes in the field and they were all got up and put in the clamps for the winter – that was another big job. All the potatoes that were not edible, we used to chop up roughly into chunks. That was done by the women who worked on the farm. We used to have to put a little tiny bit of potato by each strawberry plant. You would push it in the earth under the plant because wireworms attack strawberry plants but they go for the potato before the strawberries. So, you would put the little bits of potato down and leave them there for a few days and then you would go back and pick them all up and they would be full of wireworms. You would just kill all the wireworms and put the potato back again and this was the way of keeping the wireworms from attacking the strawberries. Looking back now it is quite amazing to think that there was a team of women in the strawberry field going up and down all day putting these little bits of potato by the plants to clear the plants of wireworm. We used to have a little sharp knife to thrust them all through and kill them all and put the potato back again. I couldn't imagine anyone, for one thing being paid these days to do a job like that, or even having the patience to do it because it was a terribly monotonous job. I don't know what they do these days to get rid of pests like that. I should imagine they just spray them all, so again you are coming back to chemicals. Then we didn't have the chemicals.

When we had got over this little period of clearing the wireworms, the next thing was the plants had to be strawed to keep frost off them. The tractor would go along then and put the bales of straw around the field. Then the women would have to go and get the straw but the men would come along first of all and undo the bales and get the pitchforks and loosely scatter the straw all over the strawberry plants, over the whole area that was grown. The women had to come along on their knees and you would get your two hands and push all the straw around underneath the leaves of each plant. You had to go round each plant and push the straw gently – it had to be done gently so that you didn't knock the blossom at all or any fruit that was forming. The idea of this was to keep the frost off the plant because the plants were so near to the ground – if you had some very severe frosts in the spring, they would just kill all the buds and they would go black and you wouldn't get the fruit. So it used to pay to do this. This was another really monotonous job but it was always done. You would go up and down all day pushing the straw thickly round the little strawberry plants. I don't even know if they still do this now but I have been strawberry picking for myself on farms that do pick-your-own and I notice that some of them have a bit of straw round and some don't, so I don't really know if they still do it but it used to pay us dividends to do that sort of thing.

When the fruit was ready, the same women would go picking the strawberries and that again was another little art. I think the majority of farmers would just pick but when our women picked the fruit they were not allowed to touch the fruit by hand. You had to nip the stem through with your nail, then put it in the basket that way and you didn't handle the actual fruit. When you handle a strawberry it bruises very easily and if it is bruised – although you don't notice it the day you pick it – by the next day it would be all mushy. I think that is why our fruit used to go up to London to be sold and why it was always in such good condition because if you see fruit in the shops it is not very often you see strawberries that look really nice and fresh with that lovely gloss on them – a perfect fruit. In the daytime my mother used to go out into the shed and pack this fruit all up, with a team of women doing all the work. About three or four women worked in the shed packing the fruit all day and it was all untouched by hand – what patience and it looked lovely, all in these two pound punnets and then put into crates. Then the lorry would turn up, just an ordinary big lorry, open-backed with a big tarpaulin that went over the top and that was all loaded up and everybody knew everybody. The haulage man was another friend and had always done that sort of work for us and it was all loaded up and taken off up to London and sold in Covent Garden. The comments that we had come back about the quality of the fruit made all the work that went into it worthwhile.

At weekends we used to sell some of the fruit by the roadside. We started off by just having an ordinary kitchen table put out near our front gate and we put some punnets of fruit out there for sale and gradually it became a bigger thing. Eventually one end of the packing shed was opened up and we had fruit in there that we sold. It was not cheap according to the prices in those days – we didn't sell it cheaply but people didn't mind what they paid because they said they were getting really good fruit for their money. They would not go and pay a lower price and get something that was mushy or not fresh. The people that mostly bought the fruit by the roadside were the people that came down to the country for the weekend from London. Certain families would come down to the countryside for a day out or go on down to the coast. They would pop in and see the fruit and buy it and it became an outing for them to come down from London to our farm, buy the fruit and go back again and have their strawberry-and-cream tea. Some of them even used to have a picnic tea of strawberries and cream because we started selling cream as well to go with it.

We also supplied a shop in Tenterden with fruit, so it didn't all go to the London markets, but we were very well known for the quality of the fruit. They used to have the annual fruit show at Marden every year and we always put in apples and we nearly always got the first prize – we had cups and medals. And the strawberries went into a show and we were always getting prizes for them so it proved that it did pay. We didn't do all of this just to get prizes at shows, that wasn't the aim. The aim was top produce, a good well-flavoured fruit, but it did prove that it paid to do the thing properly.

The next thing we had was raspberries. We didn't grow quite so many raspberries, about half a field, and they were sent up to London and sold locally as well. We had a few loganberries and one small orchard of plums. They were also picked and sent to the same place. There were the Victoria plums, the Czar plums and the Giant Prunes – they were the varieties we used to grow. Another thing about varieties, is that names of varieties have changed. With the strawberries, we used to grow the Royal Sovereign and Paxtons. The Royal Sovereign was a very popular variety; the Paxtons came a little bit later but the Royal Sovereign had a really beautiful flavour and I have wondered why I never see any farmers growing them these days. I was asking a farmer about it and he said they don't grow that variety now because it is a very early one. The season of growing it isn't very long whereas the other ones carry on a bit longer. It was such a lovely flavoured fruit and a very popular one and I just don't know why they stopped having that particular variety.

Now when I go to a fruit farm to pick my own strawberries, there are so many different varieties I find myself asking the farmer what they are for – which one is best for eating and which is best for jam? They have got certain varieties these days that they recommend for jam-making and other ones for eating, whereas with the Royal Sovereign we used to use the smaller ones at the end of the season for jam-making and the better ones for eating. You wouldn't start making jam until the end of the season when you had the small fruit but it doesn't seem to apply now because they just have a special variety for jam. This also goes for the plums: I know the Czar plums are still around now, as well as the Victoria. I am not sure about the Giant Prune but that was a harder plum. But there are a lot more varieties now than what there used to be when we were farming.

Another thing we grew were blackcurrants and they were enormous. The blackcurrant bushes were grown between the plum trees so that was how they spaced things out – you had the tall trees and the bushes. We had blackcurrants and a few redcurrants. They all had to be picked – that was quite a tedious job – then they were sent up to London. I have never seen blackcurrants like them; they were half the size of a cherry, but they were beautiful and juicy.

When they had got over the blackcurrant picking it would be the start of the apples and that was a very long season because we would start off with one of the early varieties. I have a list of them: there were Bramleys, Millers, Laxton Superb, Fortunes, James Greeve, George Cave, Worcesters, Red Miller and Monarchs and the Cox's Orange Pippins, of course. These were all the different varieties that we used to have. I think that the James Greeve was the earliest one, then the Millers and so it went on. We were particular about picking the apples. You had to put your hand under the apple, gently hold it with a little twist and it would come off in your hand and you placed it into your basket. You never dropped it and you didn't squeeze it or press it so you never had any finger-marks on it and so there was no bruising. The strange thing is when you know how to pick fruit and you are shown the correct way to pick it, if you stick to that it becomes so easy it doesn't take any longer than pulling it off the tree like a lot of people do, and mishandling it so you get bruised fruit. They were all picked that one way and they certainly kept very well. All this fruit was picked and taken again into the packing shed and in the days when I was small and at school, we hadn't got all the equipment that we had later on so they were just taken into the shed and packed and put into these boxes. They were all taken up to London to the markets or to the shop in Tenterden or some sold at the door again.

While this activity was going on, all through June, July and August the hay-making was continuing, so the work had to revolve between the lot. You can imagine what a busy time it was with the harvesting. The stockmen were looking after all the cattle, including the pigs. That was another industrious side of the farm because we had a very large herd of pigs which we used to breed and, of course, a lot of the skimmed milk from the butter was mixed in with the pig food – that was one outlet for it. It was quite a paying thing to have pigs then.

During the summer months you were so busy you were literally up in the mornings and working right through until you went to bed at night. You had all the lovely summer weather but you didn't have much chance to take advantage of relaxation. Holidays were not really bothered about because everyone was so busy working. That was the time of the year when you reaped the benefit of what you had put in. One thing was interwoven with another and all the different crops that we grew had to weave in with one another, so that they could all be dealt with at the right times.

Later on we had a big cold storage built and a proper packing shed for the apples. We had a big grading machine and everything so then, of course, the apples were picked and taken into that shed and they were run on the grader and put into cold storage. We could keep them all through the winter for the Cox varieties, the longer keeping ones. We entered them in shows and, of course, when they were put in shows we used to polish them up with a soft cloth and put them all in the boxes. They looked really lovely – the colours that came up when you polished them. I think it was lovely seeing so much fruit around and they were so crisp and juicy and the flavour of them was delicious. We did spray them. They were sprayed at regular times of the year but I wish I could remember how many times. I think it was only twice a year but it may have been more because I wasn't very old then and I cannot remember exactly. Nowadays they seem to be spraying them an awful lot. I don't know what they use but I can't help thinking it must make a lot of difference to the flavour of the fruit because I think something is terribly wrong in the methods of fruit growing now. All the fruit was packed into containers: with some it was punnets, with some it was chips, with others it could be boxes or crates. When you had filled one up you stacked it into heaps and then the men would come along and move the heaps to where the tractor could get to them. The tractor would run down the centre between the trees and load them all up onto the trailer and drive straight back to the packing shed. A horse could do it: they had done it in the early days but not for very long because they obviously would be a lot more cumbersome to get down between the apple trees. The tractors seemed a slimmer line of thing to do but we still had jolly good use of horses anyway.

When the apples were finished that was the end of the fruit for that year. When they were all picked then the orchards were cleared. I think various things were done to the trees: probably spraying before Christmas but they were more or less left again until we started on the routine with pruning and picking up prunings again. So there was a circle that went from Christmas round to Christmas. In the winter when we had the big cold store and packing shed, then very often my father was in the barns in the evenings in the winter with Tilley lamps preparing and packing the fruit. If we had anything special we wanted the fruit for, he would get it out and see to it. I have known him to be working down in that barn in the evenings in the winter for hours. It was a full-time job.

In 1939 I left school and there was a rumour of the war coming. I worked on the farm at the time. My mother had a terrific lot of work to do in the house and needed more help – she really needed me there. So I was partly spending my time helping her in the house and then going out and helping on the farm. I did this, and then when the war started, of course, I was needed more on the farm. So I was working out in the fields then a lot. I would help my mother in the house for a couple of hours and then go out the rest of the day and help on the farm, so I got to know more about the farm. I was doing a lot of things. I did the budding I was telling you about and the pruning, the strawberries and all this sort of thing. So I got even more knowledge then.

Another one of the things I did was to take on all of the chicken rearing. I had well over a hundred chickens and we had all the chicken houses down in one of the fields. The chickens were just running about in the field and they were completely free. They used to run into the nest boxes in the house and lay their eggs, then went back out in the field again and that is how chickens should be able to live. I used to have to go out and feed them in the morning and collect up the eggs. Then I would go back and feed them later in the afternoon and collect any more eggs. I had to clean the houses out and then every so often the houses had to be moved along because all of the chicken manure went down through the slats in the floor onto the grass. This way you gradually got the field fertilized. We would put all the chicken houses in one field at one side and gradually move the houses all over that field. When we had covered the field, we would move them to another field because that would all help to fertilize the land. This was where the horses came in. We would harness the horse up and take it out with some chains and put these on the chicken houses and then it would just walk along and pull the house to where I wanted it. A simple operation and very simply done too.

At night we used to have to go down just before dusk and shut the chickens up because of foxes. If you didn't shut them up the foxes would get them. There was an occasion when I was going somewhere one evening and someone else had said they would shut the chickens up for me and when I went down to open them up again in the morning, I was absolutely horror-struck as everywhere I looked there were dead chickens. Apparently the person that was going to shut them up had forgotten that they were supposed to do it, so they hadn't been shut up and the fox had got in there overnight and had cleared them all. I didn't have any chickens left. They don't just kill them, they tear them to pieces and then they are thrown all over the place and just left. So it is not exactly killing for the want of the food, it is killing for the sake of killing. That is the thing I always say about foxes – lovely little creatures but so cruel. After that we always did make sure they were never left again.

I used to see to the chickens that had to be reared. I used to put down the eggs first of all. I had a few hens sitting on eggs and they would hatch out and we would have the baby chicks. I used to have the hens in a big pen and have little coops all round and I would put the eggs in there. Then when I saw a chicken that was broody, I would catch her and sit her on some eggs. When they hatched out, it was really lovely to see all the little yellow bundles running about. When they got big enough to go out of this run, they would be put out in the field with the others. It is a lovely sight to see the little yellow things running around – so different from all the battery things that you have now. Later on I had a larger amount so we had one big house where all the hatching was done. It was a lot of hens in there sitting on a lot of eggs but when they had the young they would still have this run to run around in. Then eventually they would all end up out in the field. Rhode Island Reds and Light Sussex were the two breeds we used to have. I think the one thing that is terrible that has been changed is that chickens should be able to have a natural life and they should be able to run about. To see them in these batteries these days! The battery hens know nothing of life; they are just hatched, fattened up and killed. It just doesn't seem right! We also miss all that lovely pleasure of seeing the little baby chicks running around. It is very seldom you can go around to a farm these days and see a chicken about. It is quite an event when you can. I had a lot of pleasure out of rearing these little chicks and I used to look after them right up till the time I left the farm. I think that people miss out on things with all this modernization. You have to modernize, I know, and a lot of it is an improvement but some of it isn't, and battery farming is one of those things.

Another job that I used to do on the farm, with all the other women that used to work there in the winter months, was what we termed as thistle spudding. The thistles grow in fields in collections. I remember my father coming in and saying, 'There is a whole lot of thistles coming up in the First Brook [which was one of the fields]. You had better go down there and get them out.' As soon as thistles get any seed on them they spread rapidly with the wind blowing the seed, and they are very difficult to get rid of. If you get them all in the hay, it is not a good thing and if you get a farm overrun with thistles it is a very bad thing. We used to have to do that with a hand tool. You cannot use a tractor because you cannot go and turf up all your grass, so we used to have to go and take a little implement that was called a 'thistle spudder'. It was like a long handle with a little cutter thing on the end. Father put all the women on this one large area where all the thistles were. You would find a bunch of thistles and then perhaps a patch of grass where there were hardly any and then you would find another bunch. We had to go all over the fields like that. You had this little spudder and you chopped down into the ground under where the thistle was, so it cut right through the root, then root the thistle out and put it on top of the ground to dry out and die. I have to pinch myself to realize we did really do it.

It was another job that was so tedious and took a long time and yet you were paying several women to do that work, so it shows what the wages were like then. If there was no other work for the women to do then they would go out and do another lot of thistles because it was something that filled in the time when they hadn't anything else that was important to do. I know it is never done these days but, I imagine the same as most other things, it is probably done by spraying weedkillers over the thistles.

There were lots of little things I can recall which happened. Having the War on made a big difference but the amazing thing was we were where the Battle of Britain was being fought. There were air raids continually during that time and a lot of activity going on and yet it didn't matter how many air raids there were. We had incendiaries on our Dutch barn setting it alight and we had land mines on the farm. We had a German plane come down on the farm and we captured the young pilot. All these things were happening but the amazing thing was that life never seemed to alter – the work still got done to the same routine and it never really put people out. It was typical of the people of those days; they just got up and carried on their work as if nothing was happening. When a little catastrophe was over, they all went back and carried on where they left off and nobody made much fuss about it. We used to have a lot of troops stationed round the various places near us and a lot moving through. They used to have manoeuvres; big convoys of lorries would go by and it was nothing to have them stop and come in and say they needed the farm to stay in overnight. They would sleep in the hay barn or anywhere and in the very cold winter I have known my mother to have a lot of them in the farmhouse and she would put them up – it was more like a hotel for them. It amazes me to think that they were completely strange people but her attitude was that they were men that were fighting for us. She used to have them in and out would come the soup pot or any cooking and she would make them a meal. They used to have a very enjoyable time although they were on manoeuvres. I think they quite enjoyed it. It was always an open house for them all and, of course, as they couldn't all get in the house, a lot of them were in the barns, but she made sure they were comfortable.

Another thing that I remember very well were the workhouses of those days. There was a workhouse at Cranbrook and another at Tenterden. There is a seven-mile gap between them. There were lots of tramps on the roads then. Where have they all gone to? There must be some around but where are they? I don't know – probably accumulating in London in the cardboard boxes, poor things. In those days it seemed as if they had a routine; for example, stay at Cranbrook Workhouse overnight, leave that one in the morning and walk to the Tenterden one and stay there the next night. Then leave that one and go on to the next one. It was like a chain walking round the country from workhouse to workhouse where they could stay overnight. So it was quite a common sight to see the tramps walking by our place from one workhouse to the other. In the summer you wouldn't take much notice of them. If it was very hot and my mother saw them, she would ask them in and give them a cold drink or whatever they wanted. In the winter when the weather was very bad it was quite an ordinary thing to see them going by and she would call them in – they would have some hot soup or hot drink and something to eat. She would always take them in the kitchen and give them something and get chatting to them. The amazing thing was that some of them were well-educated people who had just gone onto the roads. I never knew why. I never knew if she asked them more. I was too young then to really get involved but I just remember these people. I do remember one young man in particular. He came from a well-to-do family but he had thrown everything up that he owned and taken to living on the roads. The difference I am pointing out is then they were just tramps but you could ask them into your house and trust them. Nowadays you would be afraid to ask anyone into your house. You would probably think, 'I wish I could ask that poor devil in and give him a nice hot drink' when it was a bitter cold day but you wouldn't dare do it because you wouldn't know who you were letting in. What a shame the change of times. What a shame that all the trust has gone out of us and people make us like it. I wish we could go back to how we would treat one another then.

With regard to the attitude to the boss, there was a very marked difference to what there is now. As a child, right up until I left home and probably still extended on because it just didn't arise afterwards, I was never allowed to call an adult by a Christian name. It was always Mister or Missis or Miss and treat them with respect. It was unheard of to ever call an adult by a Christian name. The owner of the farm was always addressed as Mister. My father was always addressed as Mister by all the farm workers. He used to call the people that worked for us by their names: the men by their Christian names but all of the women that worked for us, he would call them by Miss or Mrs so-and-so. It was never Christian names there. The rather quaint thing that stood out in my mind was that my mother had some friends that she had known for years and they lived near us. They had come to the house as her friends but I suddenly realized one day quite recently that I never once heard her call them by their Christian names. One particular lady was her friend for years and my mother always called her Mrs Fowler, never by her Christian name. It was one day when I was talking to my daughter that I said about her Grandma and Mrs Fowler and she said how stranger to think that Grandma called her friends Missis and not by their Christian names. She had noticed it even before me, probably because I had been brought up that way. I hadn't noticed it so much. Nowadays nearly everyone is called by their Christian name: when you work in offices it is Christian names. That is a very marked difference, I think. In those days it was always done as a sign of respect. I don't know whether that was a good thing really; I suppose it is nice to have a respect for someone but I think if you work well for anybody it is not that necessary. I think that the main thing is a good relationship between the boss and the work people and vice versa. I think maybe you are more relaxed when you use Christian names to people – it gives a completely different atmosphere to a place. I remember when we were in the fields and my father appeared or the owner appeared, where people had been working but just chatting to one another, they suddenly went quiet and there was a hushed silence until the person who had arrived had spoken and gone. Then they would resume with a more casual air. That is the sort of thing I think isn't always that good because it causes tenseness and a completely different atmosphere and I think it is better to work without that.

I cannot tell you what the wages were on the farm in those days. I know they were very low. I worked for my father and I used to help a lot in the house. My pay was worked out differently. I really didn't get proper pay – it was more like pocket money. That was one of the main reasons why I left home in the end because I wasn't getting much money. When the women were doing fruit picking they were paid by the hour, not by piece-work. A lot of people doing that type of work are paid by piece-work. We wouldn't do it because we said if they were hurrying to pick a lot of fruit to get more money they wouldn't pick the fruit properly so we kept giving them an hourly rate.

I continued to work on the farm throughout the war years until 1944 and then I left and went to work in the GPO as a telephonist. I loved the farm but it wasn't a very satisfactory arrangement. I was becoming more of a standby to help in the house and not doing as much work on the farm as I would have liked to have done. Anyway I did leave at that time and took up a different sort of work altogether. Then I went to work in the town. I often wonder how I took to working in the town but I did and I quite enjoyed it. I always kept my love of the country, always took an interest in it and was glad to go back to it, and now I am retired I find it even more so.

CHAPTER FIVE

ANGLESEY LIFE

Mrs Gwladys Williams gives a view of life in the Anglesey countryside.

I was born on 23 April 1911 at Teilia, Cemaes Bay, Anglesey. I am now a retired farmer's widow.

I went to school at the County Primary School at Cemaes, which had no water-supply apart from a cold-water tap for the whole school, coal fires and no school meals. The boys had a plot to grow potatoes, etc. As it was near the beach they used to cart seaweed up in barrows to use as fertilizer which was very good. We had a good headmaster. Some of the pupils were quite brilliant but not many sat the exam to go to the County School as few parents from the village could afford to send their children there because it meant going by bus and train and paying for lodgings in the town. It was a pity really. We only played in the playground but we used to go looking for flowers and plants near two forests close by.

There was a milk round in the village when I was young, and they used to go to villages with pony and trap. They had a big can and supplied the villagers from it with a large vessel. When I was twelve, I used to go to the furthest end of the village, carrying two cans of milk – this was a walk of about a mile and a half. I used to measure out the amount of milk the villagers wanted. Now the milk is delivered by van in bottles.

I left school at fourteen and went to work at fifteen at a private house close by. We kept a cow and poultry there. The master had a farm nearby and I used to go and help the housekeeper when there used to be a dozen or so men there for meals. Now they have a combine harvester so they don't need so many men. Most of the work was done with horses; not many people had a tractor. They grew mostly corn, barley and potatoes. I received 5s. a week with accommodation and food which was really very reasonable. My relationship with the boss and his wife was good.

Now it has made a great deal of difference to the villages and the farms around as they don't need so many people to work on them. Sometimes the farmers don't have anyone to work for them, only their sons, etc. Now they have milking machines, tractors, combine harvesters, etc., whereas most people milked by hand years ago. We used to milk the cows, feed the calves and make the butter before they had the separators and used the skimmed milk for the pigs.

There was no electricity on the farms, so it was hard work and very dark in the evenings, feeding the animals and milking. They had only paraffin lamps everywhere to light the sheds, or candles.

The farm workers used to get up about 5 o'clock in the morning and feed the horses before they went into the fields. They used to come for their cup of tea about 8 o'clock. Then they wouldn't come home often till eight or nine at night. They generally had very good meals at midday and a snack at teatime. Some bosses were not so good as others with meals. They used to have butter-milk and bread for their breakfasts in the morning.

Some people had their own meat, mostly salted beef and bacon. All the farmers' wives made their own bread and they had plenty of butter on their bread. I used to go helping some boss's wife to make jam and a lot of things for the farmhouse because it brought in a bit of money.

My husband was paid £1 a week, plus a cottage on the farm and also potatoes with free milk every day. He used to be a ploughman and he was very interested in his horses. He was very good at ploughing and used to go in for ploughing matches. He would decorate his horses and took a great deal of pride in them. I have a silver cup that he won for ploughing and several other prizes.

I don't remember many snowstorms around here but when we did get one, it was very bad for the animals which had to be kept in the barns. There was no water in the barns so we had to carry all the water from the well for them all.

Work on the farm was hard: corn was often cut by scythe, sheep-shearing with a little implement with one man turning the handle until they had shearing machines driven with petrol or electricity. Before we married, my husband used to be with the horses until bedtime, cleaning and feeding them. Nowadays, big carriers come for the cattle, sheep and horses but in those days the men had to walk many miles to market with the animals. Killing for man and beast!

The hay harvest used to be got together with forks, making the hay into haycocks and then carting them loose on the carts. The farm labourers were good at making the stacks. My husband was good at that job and thatching them too.

We were married in 1933 and after a few years on the farm, we went to a smallholding. It was very rocky and not easy to get much corn or other crops from it. So he used to go out sheep-shearing in the spring to get a bit of money and that was very hard work. During the Second World War he used to go out rabbit catching and we used to sell them to a wholesaler from Liverpool who used to come for them twice a week. Sometimes we would get 1s. a couple for them. He used to go to different farms and carry them home on his bike and on his back. We had no car but later he had a motorbike and then a tractor. Lambing-time was very hectic and there were many losses. The farmers used to get together and help each other when needed.

The seasons of the year, I think, were like now mostly. Somehow it seems that in those days we had blazing sunshine most days, or so it seems to me. We used to carry the corn at night when it was a harvest moon in September. We really had plenty of fun in the harvest time. At Christmas time most farms had lots of geese – not many turkeys around our district then. There were goose feathers floating around for a long time after all the men had been doing the 'feathering' for the day.

I do not like the hens in batteries or pigs and calves in such small places today. It doesn't seem natural but this is how most farmers survive these days, I suppose.

I used to like making our own butter. I never did make any cheese. We used to feed the pigs on the buttermilk. There are not many farm workers about now – it doesn't seem so personal any more. In those days we really were poor but didn't know about being otherwise as we were all in the same boat.

My husband did a lot of fishing too as we lived by the sea and living on the Irish Sea we had many a disaster around our rocks. The lifeboat and coastguards were out very often. I used to see the lifeboat being launched with great excitement, although lives were at risk. The best thing about these later years are the helicopters which save so many people around our coast and mountains.

There is a village school not far from here and after the children are eleven they go to the comprehensive. They always get good transport, not like we used to when we were young. We had to walk miles to school. Today they have every facility: good meals, and in the comprehensive they have swimming baths and facilities for all games. The children are very well provided for.

Village life has changed since the days gone by. There are more shops and supermarkets which most people go to now and the little shops are going out of business. There are plenty of houses being built around here. Not many have gone to ruin in the country as visitors come and make them up mostly. Near the village we have a big nuclear power station which supplies the area with electricity which is a great boon to everybody. So there is not so much unemployment around the village and they get a good wage from the power station.

CHAPTER SIX

A GLOUCESTERSHIRE FARM WORKER

Mrs Sybil Longhurst shows a keen appreciation of the wildlife of the Gloucestershire countryside.

My date of birth is 27 January 1919. I was born in the Gloucestershire village of Sherborne; so too were my father and his father and grandfather. My mother was born in the adjoining village of Windrush; also her father and grandfather. The village of Sherborne is situated 1 mile north of the A40, approximately halfway between Northfleet in Gloucestershire and Burford in Oxfordshire. It has always been an area of agriculture and is mentioned in the Domesday Book. It is recorded that in 1485 as many as 2,900 sheep were sheared in the Holding, as the village was then referred to. This was during the Cotswold woollen trade. At this period the monks of Winchcombe Abbey were the beneficiaries of the wealth from the wool, a lot of which was shipped to France.

Father was an agricultural worker and was employed on the same farm all his life. His father was also an agricultural worker and he too worked on one farm all his life. Mother did not have a regular job outside the home. She would help at the farm when the housekeeper was on holiday, such as getting a meal for the farmer and setting and skimming the milk.

I am one of six children in the family. I have three older brothers, and one brother and sister younger than me. We all had a very happy childhood and looking back I realize how very fortunate we were in having such wonderful parents. Mother was an excellent cook and a very thrifty woman, making most of our clothes often from articles picked up at jumble sales. I never once remember going hungry.

Father was a very easy-going person and an excellent gardener. He always grew plenty of vegetables, fruit and flowers and loved to enter his produce in the Annual Flower Show, collecting a few prizes especially for his treasured sweet peas. He rarely visited a public house; actually we never had one in the village but a social club was opened approximately seventeen years ago. Mother would make home-brewed beer from dried dandelion heads and packets of malt and hops, which we were allowed to sample in small quantities. Father smoked very little – a small packet of cigarettes would last him a week.

I attended the village Church of England school until I was eleven years old, when I moved on to Westwoods Grammar School in Northleach. For the first three or four years I had to cycle a distance of approximately four-and-a-half miles along the notorious A40 but, needless to say, there was very little traffic along there during the early 1930s. We had to attend school on Saturday mornings from 9 a.m. to 12 o'clock. I played netball and hockey during the winter months and tennis and cricket in the summer. I was in both the school hockey and tennis teams and excelled in sports more than academic studies. I left school when I was seventeen and managed to acquire clerical work in different forms and retired in August 1987, having been a part-time farm secretary for thirty-nine years with three generations of the same family. I also did clerical and secretarial work for our village school for thirty-six years.

When I first left school I worked half days in the village post office and my pay was 7s. 6d. or 37½p per week. When I started my paid part-time farm secretary and school clerical jobs in 1948, I received 2s. 0d. or 10p per hour and I did two hours' work on Saturday mornings at the farm job.

During my entire childhood we had no running water or electricity in the house; the privy was in the little building down six steps from the living-room and across the back yard. Fortunately we did not have to share our little house with anyone else and our yard was entirely private, being enclosed with high Cotswold stone walls. If you have read Mollie Harris's book on *Cotswold Privies* (1984) you will get a true picture of the outside early country 'loos', as she describes them to perfection. All our water had to be fetched in buckets from a pump which stood approximately 100 yards from our cottage, so for wash-day as many utensils as possible were filled by my Father, including a copper which heated the water. This was a fixture in the wash-house, which again was down the bottom of six steps in the yard. When the washing was rinsed and mangled and ready to hang on the line for drying, it all had to be carried up the steps and through the house to be pegged on the line which stretched down the side of the garden. When a bath was required the copper was filled and heated and a tin bath was used. Fortunately the wash-house was large enough to take the bath but it was a bit cold and draughty during the cold weather. I often wonder how mother managed to have such lily-white washing and cope with having to do it all by hand and in such primitive conditions. I can well remember she was often finishing off washing the socks and stockings when we arrived home from school at the end of the day.

Ironing had to be done with steel irons heated on a bracket fitted to the front bars of the open fire. A little spit on the iron was a test to see if it was hot enough to commence. If it quickly dispersed it was just right, if it fizzled it required a little longer heating.

Cooking also had to be done on an open fire with the saucepans resting on a bracket. A small oven was built into one side of the grate and in some houses a small boiler on the opposite side provided hot water for washing and washing up, etc. In the very early days the complete meal would be cooked in one large pot. The meat dish would be a boiled beef steak pudding and the vegetables would be put into specially made string nets. I well remember cooking such a meal for my grandfather and two uncles in my early teens. This would be when my aunt, who was housekeeping for them, went on holiday.

From the late 1940s water was piped into the cottage to one tap but the mains water-supply and sewerage was later, arriving sometime during the 1960s. The electricity supply was brought into the village in 1948. Lord Sherborne's house and buildings had their own supply long before that by using a turbine engine installed in a building built on a waterfall in the nearby river. As soon as we had electricity in our cottage father purchased a washing machine which mother found a real luxury. But even this modern equipment was nothing compared to the modern-day equipment of twin-tub or automatic machine but it certainly took the drudgery out of wash-day.

Pre-1930 farm work was extremely hard and dirty work. The men who tilled the land and worked the horses worked very long hours, usually starting at 6 a.m., as the horses had to be fed, groomed and harnessed before they could be hitched up to their machines. The carters, as these men were called, would take great pride in polishing the brasses and harness, which was always done in the evening after their meal. All day long the men had to walk behind their team of horses when ploughing, drilling or harrowing, etc. in all weathers and there wasn't the opportunity of purchasing anoraks, windcheaters or overalls which are available to the present-day farm workers.

Pay, of course, was very low. My eldest brother who worked on the farm for a few years when he left school had just 7s. 0d. or 35p a week for working approximately sixty hours a week – this was in 1924. All the heavy lifting and carrying has been replaced by the use of forklift trucks. My father had to carry sacks of corn on his back, containing two hundredweight of barley and oats and two-

and-a-quarter hundredweight of wheat, up a flight of stone steps without a safety side rail to a granary, usually above wagon sheds or stables. My maternal grandfather often related the day he and his mate delivered a wagon-load of barley from the mill to the local brewery four miles away at Burford on a very hot summer's day in the late 1890s. This all had to be carried up a flight of stone steps and when they had half unloaded the wagon and were hot and thirsty, Grandfather asked the brewer if there was a chance of having half-a-pint of porter. When refused the drink he felt so angry he instructed his mate to unload the remainder of the corn just where the wagon stood and where a down pipe would have released the water should it have rained. Grampy said, 'If he had given us a drink I would have been willing to have thrown the bloody sacks over the church steeple, if he had asked me to.' Of course, the Brewer reported the incident to the miller who reprimanded Grampy but that didn't worry him too much. He was quite a character.

He was born in 1857 and left school when he was eight years old. He had to earn some money to help support his mother and two sisters, his father having been killed when he was only two years old. There was no widow's pension in those days. Incidentally, Grampy had to pay 1d. a week to attend school. His first day's work on a farm was to lead horses at plough. He would tell us he could easily walk upright under the horse's belly. He was so small but he must have been tough as he lived to be almost ninety-two.

Almost all cottagers kept a pig for killing, which was always a red-letter day, and although we hated seeing our pet pig killed, we did look forward to all the lovely tasty bits as a result. There would be chitterlings, liver, brawn, faggots, pork scratchings and lovely lard seasoned with rosemary. The pig meat, never referred to as pork, had a sweet flavour all its own. Unfortunately deep freezers were not then available so one's family and friends received a joint and repaid it when their own animal was killed. It was a wonderful sight to see bacon and hams – cured by salting usually and then put on a rack or hung on the kitchen walls to dry off until such time as pieces were cut off for use. My grandfather always said the only part of a pig not useful was its squeal. Even its bladder used to be dried and then used as a football or used by the 'Fool' in the team of Mummers which was an old country custom of play acting at Christmas time. The practice of home pig killing ceased soon after the end of the Second World War. My uncle, who had done this job for many years, ceased to operate due to new legislation brought into force.

The practice of killing rabbits in the harvest field also ceased. The male population would surround the standing corn and on the approach of the binder the rabbits would bolt, only to be chased by the men and boys wielding sticks, hoping to pick up a cheap meal. The introduction of the myxomatosis disease among the rabbits almost wiped out the entire population and so another country custom came to be past history.

When we were children our parents would take us for long walks across the fields or along the hedgerows during the warm spring, summer and autumn Sunday evenings. We would pick flowers or hunt for birds' nests and gather blackberries or crab-apples to make into jam or jelly and come home tired and hungry and devour slices of spotted dick. This, mother would have made specially from a suet dough and dried fruit and spice and put in a floured cloth and boiled for one or two hours. One favourite treat during the winter months was slices of hot dripping toast. We could purchase tasty dripping from the cook at the big house for 6d. (2¹/2p) per pound. We usually had the cottage-shaped loaves and mother would pull off the top and cut it into rounds and liberally spread with dripping.

A bacon roly-poly pudding was served up at least once a week and rabbits and pigeons were the mainstay of the meat dishes. A rabbit could be purchased for 1s. and you got 6d. back for the skin from the rag-and-bone man, and pigeons cost 4d. each. We did occasionally have roast beef with a batter pudding cooked under the beef, which, when almost cooked, would be placed on a little stand in the meat tin and the batter poured under it. We also had beef steak pies and the cheaper joints of mutton which were usually used in stews. We were never short of milk so rice puddings were regularly appearing on the meal table. So too were boiled apple and jam puddings and tarts. I can never remember Mother making chips but we had a fish-and-chip van call once a week and that was a much looked-forward to meal. During the War Mother set and skimmed the milk and made little pats of butter using a large Kilner jar in place of a churn.

Winter evenings were taken up playing cards, draughts and other board games and cutting up strips of old woollen cloth for Father to make into rugs. These were lovely and warm to the feet as the floors were covered with cold linoleum as we couldn't afford the luxury of carpets at that time.

The village of Sherborne had been an estate since 1551 when Thomas Dutton bought the estate following the Dissolution of the Monasteries. A baronetcy was bestowed upon the family in 1678 and the squire was then known as Lord Sherborne. History tells us that the Parish of Sherborne originally consisted of eight farms, ninety cottages, a mill with a bakehouse, four or five shops including a post office and a blacksmith's forge. Today only four of the farms are occupied by working farmers, the others having been sold with the land and separately to the farmhouses. We only have one remaining shop with post office included and at the present day that has been put on the market for sale but we are hoping it will be retained. Several of the cottages have been converted, two being made into one, and the forge and mill have long since gone. A number of the cottages have been sold to retired couples, commuters or weekenders.

Over the past ten years we have lost a large number of our lovely ash and beech trees with all the lovely elms completely wiped out, due to disease and old age. This has completely altered the landscape.

Pre-1930 almost all of the male population in the village was employed on the Sherborne estate as carpenters, plumbers or stone-masons, as Cotswold stone was quarried during the nineteenth century; also as painters, woodmen, keepers, agricultural workers on the tenanted farms and odd-job men around the big house. During the Second World War Lord and Lady Sherborne moved from the big house to the adjoining village and the army moved in. Over the past ten years the house and adjoining stable flats have been sold to developers who have turned it into luxury accommodation with prices well out of reach of the local inhabitants, who have gradually moved away. We have maintained our village school, winning a fight with the education authorities a few years ago, and now approximately thirty children attend, some being brought in from the neighbouring villages.

Public transport today is almost non-existent with no chance whatever of using it for any evening social activities. In the past religion paid quite an important part in rural life. We had church and chapel services in the village, also Sunday school for the children and a strong male church choir. Over the past fifty years this has gradually declined, leaving us with only one church service a month, and no chapel or Sunday school services.

Another significant change in rural life today is the declining wildlife. There are very few small birds to be seen. The few existing hedgerows just outside the village are completely devoid of any wildlife of any description. To enable the larger agricultural machines to be used effectively on the land, hedgerows have been grubbed up. It has been recorded that at least one-fifth of them have disappeared. This, coupled with the use of pesticides, has been the main cause of the decline of wildlife and destruction of the lovely wild flowers. Farmers have used pesticides to kill bugs harmful to their crops, which in turn have killed the bugs and insects necessary for the conservation of nature. Otters in our local river are completely extinct. Weasels and stoats are very rarely seen. Partridges have almost disappeared and the heron population greatly reduced owing to the destruction of the trees they used for nesting. We do have a few swans, wild ducks and geese on the river and a large quantity of jackdaws and rooks, which are quite a worry, attempting to build their nests in our chimney-tops, following the loss of the trees.

When I first started my job as farm secretary I kept the accounts, recorded the field cultivation and planting, and as the farmer was the chairman of the District Council there were letters to type, etc. Later a milking herd was introduced so there were milk records to keep. The farmer and his son were farming three rented farms from the estate and one small one they had bought, which was approximately four miles away. Just as everything was running smoothly, disaster struck in the form of the dreaded foot and mouth disease. It broke out on one of the farms where pigs were being reared. It was thought that starlings had brought the virus. The awful despondency this disease brings just has to be experienced to be believed. All the animals on that particular farm had to be killed. It didn't matter that they were nowhere near the pigs but to stop the possibility of the disease spreading, they just had to be killed. My young brother who was working on the farm at the time, had to help in their burial. I remember it made him feel quite ill for some time but work had to go on and in time things gradually got back to normal.

The breeding of turkeys was done on quite a big scale which resulted in a lot of work being done in a short time. All the farm employees and a few extra part-time females would help to pluck the birds. The bulk of the work was done in the evenings. It was a dirty smelly job but we all had great fun doing it, swapping tales and gossip. Occasionally things got a bit boisterous but what else could you expect with a mixed crowd who worked very well together and enjoyed a harmless prank? We were split into two groups, the majority of the men working in a shed on the farm where the turkeys were reared and the rest of us in another farmhouse scullery. We were fortified with cups of hot cocoa and so a mucky job was turned into a happy occasion.

The farm manager left and I then took over the job of doing the wages and PAYE and all that entailed. A herd of pedigree Guernsey cows was introduced, making a little extra work as there still remained the herd of Friesians. Then quite suddenly just a few days before Christmas in 1964 the senior member of the family died and the son was left to run things with his two young sons. Inevitably changes occurred and then one farm was sold and some employees had to leave. Within three years the son also died after a short illness. Great sorrow was felt and drastic changes then took place. The estate agents decided the three rented farms should be divided into two working units and a new farmer was allowed to move into one of the farms. The workforce was now very much reduced and many sad times followed. There were now only five people working on this farm in spite of it having an increased acreage, whereas as in 1924 the workforce totalled sixteen. A good example of how the introduction of machinery had drastically reduced the labour force! The milking herds had been sold some time previously, pigs were never reintroduced after the foot and mouth disease, and turkey and poultry rearing was wound up. Young calves were bought in when a few days old and rearing them for beef was introduced. The farmyard was completely changed: most of the animal boxes were taken out to be replaced by large sheds to winter the cattle. All the rick-standings were demolished to make room for corn-storing silos and drying plants, etc.

There is a saying 'like father like son' but in the case of our family it was 'like father like daughter'. My father received the long service medal for working over forty years on the same farm. It was presented to him by the late Duke of Gloucester at the Three Counties Show in 1959. I received my long service medal for working thirty-nine years in September 1987 at the Moreton-in-the-Marsh One-Day Agricultural Show, thus ending an era of long-standing family work in agriculture as none of the remaining family is thus employed.

At rest by the haystack

Mrs Alice Stacey with fellow workers on a farm in Bexley, Kent, in 1934

Scything the headlands, c. 1910. To make room for the reaper the corn had to be cleared from the headlands. The man on the right is cutting the corn using a scythe; the women are gathering it up and tying it into sheaves. Scenes like this were common until the introduction of the combine harvester (Park)

Shocking up. Eight sheaves were leant together leaving a little tunnel through the middle so that the wind could blow through and dry the corn more rapidly (Poole)

A break in the harvest field (Brooks)

A farm worker's cottage in the Cambridgeshire Fens (H. Bye)

83

War workers, 1914–18 (Mrs Longhurst)

Women workers, c. 1914 (from an old postcard)

A pony and cart, c. 1905 (Toulson)

The village shop, 1910 (Toulson)

The parlour maid (Wallis)

Harvesting cauliflowers, 1938 (Newling)

Potato picking, Whitlesey Fen, 1938 (Ellington)

Milking by hand

Women workers in the hay field, c. 1914–18 (Park)

Women helping with haymaking during the First World War (Park)

The new tractor

CHAPTER SEVEN

EAST ANGLIAN MEMORIES

Mrs Janet Hughes from East Anglia gives an insight into the family life of a farm worker in Suffolk and later in Essex during the 1920s and '30s.

I am Janet Hughes, born Janet Welham on 16 January 1911 at Battisford, a village near Stowmarket in Suffolk. My father was a horseman on a farm in the village and my mother was in service in the farmhouse where my father was employed. They married and spent most of their married life in Battisford. When the farm was sold in the 1920s he worked for the British Acetate Silk Corporation. When this firm closed down in 1930 he started a small haulage business and continued with this until he retired.

I was one of a family of four, having three brothers, one older and two younger. I went to a council elementary school in Battisford, leaving at the age of fourteen-and-a-half years. This school is now used as a community centre and the village children go to a neighbouring village school. On leaving school I went into service in the village for five months. I was now fifteen years old and moved to another family in an adjoining village for two years. I was paid £1 a month, being paid on the first of each month which meant I received £12 a year, plus my food. Just before my seventeenth birthday I was given notice to leave as the farmer had become bankrupt. This farmhouse was demolished and the land taken over by the Ministry of Defence before the Second World

War, when the Wattisham Royal Air Force Station was built. Honeypot Cottage, where my great aunt and uncle lived, was demolished at the same time.

I decided I would like a change of work and the vicar of our parish arranged for me to work without pay in a solicitors' office in Needham Market. This enabled me to learn general office work while also learning shorthand and typing. After six months I worked in the wages office of the silk works in Stowmarket until it closed down in the spring of 1930. Due to the depression no jobs were available and I was forced to go on the dole. I received 12s. 10d. per week, this being just under 65p. In September of that year I married Albert Hughes, a shepherd, and moved to Pebmarsh, a small village in Essex.

In my childhood we lived in a cottage on the Straight Road in Battisford – this road being straight for a mile. As a child I can vividly remember a horse running away. Hearing an awful noise I looked up the road and saw the horse and cart galloping in my direction. I rushed into the garden and shut the gate; I was very frightened. As it went by I saw it was the village undertaker taking the coffin to the home of a small child drowned while playing in a meadow. I can still recall the look of terror on his face. Fortunately at the end of the road, the horse was confronted with a very high hedge and as the road was so straight he could see this well in advance and pulled up soon enough for the undertaker to take control and safely turn the corner. Sometime after this a horseman was killed while ploughing when his horses ran away when frightened by the huntsman's horn with the hunt and hounds in full cry. For some unknown reason he was unwilling or unable to let go of the reins. Another man was killed on Christmas Day driving his pony and cart. His wife wasn't thrown out and was able to explain that the horse had been frightened as a pheasant rose up and flew in front of them. Another man, a farmer in this village, fell from his tumbrel onto the hard road. We tend to forget these accidents and think that there were no road accidents in the day of the horse.

The roads were very rough and stony in those days, especially the country lanes and side roads. I can remember women and children picking stones from the fields, and these being used to fill up the big holes in the roads. While I was at school, the so-called tar-pot, drawn by a horse came round spraying the roads with tar, and after gravel had been spread over, the steamroller came and rolled it down. By the late 1920s most roads were reasonably good.

Our cottage had one largish living-room with an open fireplace. Kettles and saucepans were boiled on the hobs either side and except for the baking done in the brick ovens, this was the only means of cooking. About this time the three-burner oil stoves became available but were quite expensive. We had another room with a brick floor; this was called a back-house. In here was the copper and oven, a table for baths to stand on on washing days, a long stool, called a washing stool, with bowl and soap for washing hands. Washing up was done on the table. Baking day was always Friday when the brick oven would be heated by burning faggots of wood until the bricks were red hot. Ashes were then cleaned out with an oven peel, a tool with a long handle to reach the back of the oven. Tins of bread would be put on this to put them in the right place in the oven to get the most heat. The long handle also prevented you burning yourself on the hot bricks. Bread was always baked first – a week's supply. When the bread came out, pastries, cakes, etc. would be put in. In late summer and autumn, jars of sliced pears would be stood in the oven all night and slow cooking gave them a lovely flavour.

The wood faggots came from a fence given by the farmer and cut during the winter. They were sold by the score, never individual faggots. Often a tree would also be given by the farmer to his workmen as firewood. These were cut down during the winter and sawn up, all by a hand cross-cut saw. It meant a lot of hard work each weekend by neighbours helping each other.

The only lighting throughout the house were oil lamps and candles and the chief floor covering was coconut matting. There were

ims, each with a large basin and ewer for washing yourself. Baths were taken on Saturday night in front of the fire. When
no rain-water was available, water had to be fetched from an arte-
sian well up the road. All drinking-water had to be fetched from
there as well. It had a very large handle to turn to bring up this
water – it was very heavy and took two children to turn it. We certainly learned not to waste water, knowing if you did you had to go
and fetch more! There was an outside lavatory with two wooden
seats side by side, a large high one and a small low one. This was
about twenty yards from the back door of the house. On dark
nights you would take a lighted candle in a tall glass jam jar to find
your way there. This was considered safer than a lantern as it didn't
blow out or tip over so easily.

Battisford School had three rooms. There was an infants room
with one teacher, a room for Standard I and II with one teacher
and a large room with no partition with Standard III and IV at one
end with a teacher, and at the other end with just an open space
dividing the classes, the headmistress took Standard V and VI.
There was an open fireplace in each room but no lighting. In the
porch there was a sink and roller towel but no tap water. Pails of
cold water were always there each morning so I presume the care-
taker had to fetch these from the well. The boys' playground was
parted from the girls' by high iron railings. PT, then called drill,
took place on the concrete square of the boys' playground.
Everywhere else was shingle, though later on a part of the girls'
playground was concreted. Both were very hard on your knees
when you fell down and even harder on the knees of the stockings.

Playtime was spent skipping, playing hopscotch, sometimes 'five
stones' or marbles according to season and weather. Ring games
were played all the time. When playing marbles, it was not
unknown for tears to be shed at the loss of a favourite coloured
glass alley, as they were always highly prized, both because of the
lovely colour and their scarcity. After school and at weekends in
winter, we would bowl hoops and skip; in the summer it would be

spinning tops. This all took place on the road. In the dinner hour children living near enough went home, while those unable to do so brought sandwiches. These had to be eaten outside whenever the weather allowed.

Opposite the school there was a garden in which the older boys worked, while girls of the same age were taken to Needham Market for cooking lessons, travelling in a lorry that was used for delivering coal for the rest of the week, with planks of wood being put each side for seats. It was always well scrubbed out but we didn't risk putting on our white aprons and caps until we arrived in the school. We really enjoyed this trip, thinking of it as an outing. We were well taught the basic skills of cooking including all the joints of lamb, pork, beef and mutton and which to use for roasting, boiling, frying or braising. There was no grilling lesson because stoves didn't have a grill. We never hear of mutton nowadays; it is always called lamb.

For school I wore a white starched pinafore, black stockings and black button boots. Whatever happened to all the boot buttons I lost? Being sent to find a boot button was a hopeless task. I am sure the button hook used for doing up the buttons was the cause of them coming off so frequently. When at last the boots were past wearing, the buttons were taken off and stored as if they were diamonds, kept safely for the next time I was sent to look for one. I had exactly the same trouble with hair ribbons – no one lost more ribbons than I did. As soon as we arrived home from school we would have to take off school clothes and put on old ones to play in. Every so often an inspector would come to see if we had head lice or nits in our hair. We always called her the 'louse-woman'.

As the seasons changed, so did after-school activities. In spring, as the wood in the hedgerows reached the right condition, whistles would be made from ash wood, and catapults and whips for our tops from any wood available. Pop-guns were made from elder wood, so these were made in autumn, just as it reached the stage where it would have enough pith to push out to make a large le to take a pellet. These were made from acorns or chewed-up paper. Bonfire night [5 November] was always celebrated: there were no lessons that day. Instead there were games, singing and lots of refreshments, and Union Jacks everywhere. I doubt if we realized the full meaning of it but that didn't stop us looking forward to and enjoying it.

As children we always went to Sunday school, to the Congregational in the morning and to the parish church in the afternoon. This meant you had two Sunday school treats. One was held at Battisford Hall where we had games, races, competitions and tea. For the parish church treat we were taken to Needham Market where our vicar lived. It was very similar to the other one but as we were taken there by wagon and horse led by church-going farmers, we thought it was the most enjoyable. It must be remembered that in those days one seldom left one's own village. There was also a Free Church building at the other end of the village. This was called the Tin Room or Tin Meeting because it was built of sheets of tin. Mr Harwood of the hall built it for them. He also provided the Sunday school building for the Congregational Church. This was always called Harwood's Sunday School but it is now a bungalow. The Tin Room was burnt down in 1962 and the members raised enough money to build a new church that is now called Battisford Free Church. It has a band of about twenty musicians. Before the services they marched to the Bold Corner, held a brief service and marched back to the church and played for the service. This continues today.

At the age of eleven, I played the organ at the parish church for Sunday school and at fourteen for church services, continuing until I married. On my wedding day I was presented with a clock bought with money given by the congregation. This clock is still going and striking the hour and half-hour today, nearly fifty-eight years later.

When entering service on leaving school it was on condition I could have Sundays free to play the organ. This was a concession but it meant I always had Sundays off. When I was twelve years old I took part in a Service of Song at the Congregational Sunday school. This consisted of a story with a religious theme: a chapter would be read and then a suitable hymn sung until the end of the story was reached. During the Christmas season we were taken by horse, led by Mr Harwood, to the workhouse at One House near Stowmarket. We performed this Service of Song for the inmates as a Christmas treat. I remember the women all dressed alike in blue striped dresses and caps, sat on one side of the building and the men, all wearing shirts of the same striped material, sat on the other side. I have always remembered this as a very sad evening. They showed no emotion whatsoever and we were not allowed to speak to them and at the end they were marched out while we were given refreshments. I don't remember this but later on my parents told me that on arrival home I was very upset and crying. I was never allowed to take part again.

It was a great day when we had our first wireless – a crystal set. Tuning with a 'cat's whisker' to get a programme was quite difficult. With only one pair of headphones it was very much a case of 'take your turn'. When we later had a wireless set and loudspeaker that ran off wet and dry batteries, it was much better for everybody. Each week the wet battery was taken to be recharged and the one left the previous week collected. The charge for this was 6d. (2^1/$_2$p). At one time we also had a wind-up gramophone with a large horn.

The boys used to collect birds' eggs. They all seemed to have a collection but there still seemed lots of birds around, even more than today. The birds that there are few of today, weren't the ones that were collected. No one ever collected barn owls' eggs – even if they wanted them, they wouldn't have been able to get them. They would never take robins' or wrens' eggs because it was considered bad luck.

Each year a pig was killed but children were always taken away to visit relatives that day. I realize now that it was to avoid the sight and sound of the slaughter. Pigs were never thought of as pets but as food so it was never upsetting to discover what had happened while we were away.

Albert Hughes, my husband, was born on 3 August 1905 in Battisford. His father was a shepherd on the estate of Mr Harwood of Battisford Hall. His mother was also born in Battisford and was a maid when she married Thomas Hughes and had four children. One died of diphtheria in childhood. My husband went to the same school as I did, leaving at the age of thirteen-and-a-half due to having 'flu during the severe epidemic after the First World War. This caused some heart trouble so that when he was well enough to return to school he had passed the leaving age. Starting work at fourteen-and-a-half, he helped his father with the sheep and did some general work. He went on to become a horseman, starting work at 6 a.m. feeding the horses. He would then go indoors and have his breakfast. At 7 a.m. he would take out the horses for whatever work was to be done that day, according to the season. It could be ploughing or carting manure onto the fields in winter, drilling or horse-hoeing in spring, cutting the corn with a binder and carting it home in wagons in summer, and ploughing and drilling again in the autumn. He would work until 11 a.m. when there would be a break for 'elevenses', eaten in the fields, and then carried on until 3 p.m. Horses would then be fed and watered and then he would go home for the main cooked meal of the day and return later to let the horses out into a strawed yard in winter or onto a meadow in summer.

On 1 September 1930 my husband left Suffolk and the horses to become shepherd for Mr John Knott of Pebmarsh in Essex. Earlier that year his elder brother, Mr Ted Hughes, had left Suffolk to go to Bournemouth to be shepherd to Mr Edwin Knott, a brother of Mr John Knott. On 24 September 1930 we were married in Battisford Church and spent all our married life in Pebmarsh. I am still living in the farm cottage we moved into on 3 May 1953 from the council house. This cottage is now owned by a grandson of Mr John Knott.

When we first came to Pebmarsh we met with some resentment from the other men and their families. Snide remarks about Suffolk people were made but we very soon lived this down and became accepted and made many friends. In 1930 the pay of a shepherd was 30s. plus a free cottage. This was for looking after the sheep seven days a week. They had 9d. stopped for the National Insurance stamp. Agricultural workers didn't receive Unemployment Pay until 1936 so didn't pay for the extra stamp. Mr Knott didn't have an acceptable cottage available at the time but there were four council houses being built for farm workers when we were interviewed for the job in July 1930 and we were allocated one of these. These houses were built to a lower standard than those already on the site to allow them to be let for a rent a farm worker could afford to pay. They had no separate kitchen or coal house compared with the other houses. The rent was 4s. 9d., just under 25p. My husband's pay was increased to cover this rent in lieu of a cottage.

The relationship was one of master and workman but always pleasant and kind, with respect on both sides. In the next generation it became more relaxed and friendly. As a shepherd he was left to do his work without interference after discussion with the farmer, who came round to the men each morning on horseback – the next generation used a Land Rover.

The basic hours were from 7 a.m. to 5.30 p.m. Monday to Friday and Saturday 7 a.m. to 12 noon until 1946 when weekly hours were reduced by two hours and Saturday's working day became 7 a.m. till 10 a.m. On the death of Mr Donald Knott in March 1986 the land was divided between his two sons and they are now farming separately. In 1930 there were fourteen men employed on this estate but in 1988 one grandson had two full-time employees and the other grandson had one part-time employee, doing most of the work himself. More and larger machines are used and no farm animals are kept.

In 1930 there was an Agricultural Workers Union agent living in the village who collected the subscriptions from the men once a month and dealt with any union business, such as accidents, etc. Today no one belongs to the union and when the union called a strike a few years ago they all went to work as usual. This was after the Agricultural Union joined the Transport & General Workers Union. There are very few farm workers in the village anyway.

There was no paid annual holiday but after the lambs were sold we were always given a few days off with pay to visit our parents in Battisford. Sheep were kept in folds, set each day with iron hurdles pulled by the shepherds' pony, four at a time. When lambs were old enough they were given separate folds using wooden hurdles or sheep wire-netting. All the stakes for these had to be driven into the ground with a wooden mallet, after first making a hole in the ground with an iron fold-pitch. A lamb hurdle was included so that the lambs could return to their mothers when they wished. This hurdle had wooden rollers which the lambs soon learned to use. According to season these folds held turnips, clover, colewort, mustard, etc. Mangolds were carted to them in winter. In 1930 they were also fed locust beans but these were soon substituted by linseed cake, slabs of which were fed into a cake machine and ground up by turning a large wheel by hand.

In spring sheep were walked across autumn-sown wheat for them to eat the top growth, causing it to sprout out. This gave the sheep some fresh, green feed and at the same time firmed the ground, saving men and horses from having to roll it. On occasions sheep were taken to the churchyard to eat off the grass as no one was prepared to cut it. Many of the graves have now been levelled and old gravestones removed so that a lawnmower can be used. The sheep were also taken to a neighbouring village green and various small meadows of owners who didn't want to cut them for hay. Walking on the road helped to wear down their hooves, saving trimming of their feet. A watch was always kept for foot rot and immediately treated as otherwise they became lame very quickly.

Lambing started in March and the shepherd's hut, tortoise stove, fuel, straw and hurdles for the lambing pens were taken to the meadow chosen for lambing. My husband slept in the hut for about a fortnight during the main lambing period. At the start and end of the lambing he would visit the flock late at night and in the early morning until all the ewes had lambed. During the night he used a torch instead of the old lantern, considering it safer with so much straw around. The extra payment for lambing was 6d. (2$^{1}/_{2}$p) per lamb up to the number of ewes in the flock, and 9d. (4$^{1}/_{2}$p) for lambs above that number. Being paid after the lambs were sold you weren't paid for the number of lambs born but for the number living at the date of the sale.

The sale was in July at Braintree. The evening before the sale we would walk them to a borrowed meadow, a distance of 4 miles. Here they would rest for the night. The master would fetch us from there and return us at 4 a.m. next day. We would then walk the 8 miles to Braintree with the shepherd walking in front with his crook. The collie dog would be in charge behind and I would be going along shutting garden gates that had been left open all night, standing in field gateways and letting traffic through. This was mainly horse-drawn – very little motor traffic.

We always made sure we got through Halstead before the factories were started up or the shops opened. The streets were pretty deserted at that hour. On arriving at the sale meadow we penned the lambs and one of us stayed with them until they were sold, when they were no longer our responsibility. Approaching the meadow it was possible other flocks would be coming from other directions and that meant keeping your lambs rounded up until it was your turn to be penned. Once they got mixed up, it was very difficult to get them back under control. Arriving early was worthwhile to avoid this happening. Fortunately we didn't ever have any trouble. After the sale we came home in the master's old Ford car. Another sale was held in September for late lambs but we didn't go to this one.

In late May or early June, according to the weather, shearing would start. In 1930 this was done by a shearing gang but at the end of that season they decided, due to age, to give up shearing and we undertook to try and do it ourselves. We were paid 6d. per sheep, which included catching sheep, tying up fleece and stacking them in a barn at the end of the day. We were paid when the wool was sold and the fleeces counted. Sheep had to be dipped each year; this had to be done by law and the village policeman had to attend to ensure that the sheep went completely under the water, head and all. It was always Coopers Dip that was used – they came out looking very yellow. The sheep-dipping trough was a deep concrete trench with a ramp at each end to make it easier for the sheep to go in and out. The shepherd would press each one under with his crook as they went through.

As shepherd my husband wore cord breeches and leather buskins, called leggings in some counties, and heavy leather boots – wellingtons came later. He had a pony and cart solely for his use. The cart was made in the village soon after we came. It was rather like a light tumbrel and painted bright scarlet. It had no seats, just a board put across to sit on. He used it at the busiest times to help with extra jobs, such as fetching corn sacks from the railway station ready for harvest and returning them after the corn was sold. These sacks were hired from the railway and charged for the time you had them. If the steam ploughs came after the harvesting, he would keep them supplied with coal and water, enabling them to work until 9 p.m. He would also take the weekly ration of oats to each farm for feeding the horses.

At harvest time we shared the work of the sheep to enable the shepherd to help with harvest. Between 7 and 9 a.m. he would set the fold for the day and then I would take over. About 10 a.m. I would harness the pony and fasten him to the shafts of the cart and drive him home. After putting him in the stable or the meadow, I would cook our midday meal. About 2 p.m. I would cycle to the sheep and let them into their new fold. This meant we still received full shepherd's pay plus the hours worked in the harvest. This money helped to buy clothes for the winter. As the corn fields were cleared I would keep the sheep on the stubble and while they were feeding I would pick blackberries, nuts, crab-apples and sloes from the hedgerows. After rain there would also be mushrooms. Nothing was sprayed so everything was made use of in some way. In spring I would pick dandelions for wine.

On 5 October 1937 the sheep were sold. The evening of the 4th we walked them half-way to Sudbury, leaving them on a meadow to rest for the night. Next morning we walked them to Sudbury Railway Station and with the help of the railway staff, loaded them into cattle wagons and we boarded the passenger train to Bury St Edmunds to be there ready to unload them and take them to the cattle sale yard. After penning them, they were the responsibility of the auctioneer. We bought fish and chips for our dinner, having been given the money for this – quite a luxury! After the sale, we were brought home, rather sad to see the end of our shepherding days. Farmers were turning more and more to arable farming. Those who continued to keep sheep put fields down to grass and let them more or less look after themselves without employing a shepherd.

My husband was then asked to take charge of the pig herd but this he disliked so much he decided to leave and answered an advert for a horseman's job at Maldon. This he got and we went to Maldon and looked at the very nice house provided. Mr Donald Knott phoned Mr John Knott and then came to see us and said that although they had sent a very good reference to Maldon they would like him to stay with them. After discussion they decided to ask him if he would stay if they bought him a tractor and taught him to drive it. They would give him an extra 10s. a week. This was agreed and later he became the driver of their first combine and for this he received £10 for each harvest done.

In those days the combines had no cabs and the drivers got covered in dust. The farmer had a shower installed in an outbuilding and he was able to have a hot shower and change his clothes before coming home. I am not quite sure who appreciated it most. I was always in favour of the dust and dirt being left behind and I made quite sure he always took clean clothes, bath towel and soap each day. He continued working with machinery for the rest of his working life, having done tractor hoeing, drilling, hedge cutting, ploughing, combining and any job that needed doing, in fact.

Weekends would often be spent rabbiting with ferrets, sometimes for food and sometimes to sell, or both. Pigeons were shot and either eaten or sold. We always had a large garden and grew all our own vegetables. Main crop potatoes would be put in a clamp in the garden until the New Year. In late spring surplus parsnips, beetroot and potatoes would be made into wine. With sugar at 3d. a pound, it was quite a cheap hobby. In the winter there would be days of shooting. The men would go as beaters and receive extra money and a good lunch. But before Wellington boots and leggings were available, it could be quite uncomfortable walking through tall sugar beet and kale. There is no longer any shooting on this farm.

For several years my husband did hair cutting. Quite a few of the village boys and men came to have their hair cut for 2d. He also mended our shoes. I still have the hot iron he used, shaped with a large and small foot. From 1940 to 1946 he was a Special Constable, being on duty three or four nights each week and always having to go out if the air-raid siren was sounded, chiefly to make sure the blackout was strictly observed.

In 1930 our first home, when newly married, was a council house. The accommodation consisted of a large combined living-room and kitchen, a very tiny front room, three bedrooms, an outside wash-house and lavatory. Lighting was by oil lamp and candles. A kitchen range was provided for cooking and heating. A coal fire heated the top of the stove for boiling or frying and the oven for baking or roasting. When the heat wasn't needed for cooking it could be opened up and used as an open fire to sit by. I cooked entirely with this range until I bought my first electric cooker in 1952. Electricity came to the village in 1930. This we had immediately for lighting and radio. At that time we were only allowed to have three lights and one point installed.

Washing day was always Monday. The copper in the wash-house was washed out overnight with rain-water, whenever possible; otherwise it meant fetching water from the pump across the road. Next morning the copper fire would be lit and while the water was heating, baths would be taken down from the walls of the wash-house and placed ready and enough wood brought in to keep the fire going. When boiling was completed the clothes were sorted: the whites for boiling, coloured things and woollens – the latter were washed separately with Lux and never with washing powder. Starch would be made for tablecloths, etc. Washing and boiling completed, the two baths would be filled with clean water for rinsing, and a Reckitts Blue [block] tied up in a piece of muslin would be used to blue the water for the second rinse. This was to keep the whites a good colour. After this final rinse I used a rubber-rolled wringer fixed to the washing stool to get as much water as possible from the clothes. The tighter you screwed the rollers the drier your washing became but it was then quite hard work turning it. Some people had a large wooden-rolled mangle but I always had a wringer. This continued until I had a twin-tub washing machine and spin-drier in 1966. On a good day ironing might be done on the same day; if not, Tuesday was the day for ironing.

Friday was baking day. I cooked everything except bread. We always kept hens for new-laid eggs and each year hatched chickens, keeping pullets to lay eggs and eating the cockerels. For a long time after moving from the council house to this farm cottage, we kept Muscovy ducks, selling them as oven-ready. They were always in great demand. The most we had at one time was forty but they became so tame and such pets we didn't like to kill them so we stopped hatching any and let them die off naturally. We also kept rabbits but not for long. I wasn't too keen on having to go collecting rabbit food in the 1930s – there were no rabbit pellets.

Pebmarsh is a small village just over the border from Suffolk. In the 1930s there were village pumps from where you had to fetch your drinking-water and for everything else when there was no rain-water. This often meant it had to be fetched for washing day. We were lucky as we had the council house near the pump but some people had quite a long way to carry it. During the summer it was quite usual for there to be a queue on Sunday evening, with baths and pails waiting their turn. A few people had their own well and pump on their property. One farmer had a water-wheel worked by the wind while others had a small engine to pump theirs. Mains water came to the village in the late 1950s and later mains sewerage as well.

In 1930 I fetched my milk and butter from the farmhouse and continued to do so for many years. I would have one pint of sepa-rated milk for 1d. and one pint of full cream, always called 'new milk', for 2d. The cream from the separated milk was churned into butter once a week. A milkman soon started a milk round, deliver-ing with a pony and cart. The milk was ladled into the customer's jug by half-pint or one-pint metal measures. As time went on it was delivered in bottles and by a motor-driven milk float. This contin-ues today. One milkman delivers six days a week and the Co-op seven days a week.

There were four bakers delivering bread, flour and cakes three days a week. We now have one who also brings dairy produce, veg-etables, fruit, confectionery, soft drinks and much more, three days a week on Tuesday, Thursday and Saturday. There was a mobile fish van on Thursdays also carrying fresh fruit and vegetables – very much the same as we had in 1930 from a fish man delivering by pony and cart. But, of course, the large mobile van can bring a much wider selection. There were three butchers delivering twice a week, taking orders in advance for the next delivery. In 1988 there was one mobile butchery van on Tuesdays and Fridays but he didn't take orders. Instead of three coal merchants delivering each week there is one delivery each Monday. Compared with most villages we are very well served in this respect.

Local GPs from two group practices held surgeries in the village twice a week but no longer do so. There was a general store and a sub-post office and shop but the general store has been closed for some years and is now a bungalow residence. The post office and shop remain, as well as the adjoining garage. Living in the village was a blacksmith with a smithy, carpenter, wheelwright, well-sinker, undertaker and thatcher. The thatcher is the only one still here: the Potter family, having done this for generations, is being carried on by two sons and their sons. Recently two young men have started up as builders and decorators. Until 1924 there was a harness-maker and saddler in the village. His granddaughter, a great friend of mine for many years, tells me as a small child she spent many hours watching him stitch horse collars and making harnesses. After harvest, he would go round to the various farms and for a small fee would examine all the harnesses to make sure they were safe for the horsemen to use, taking away any that needed repairing. The thatched cottage where he lived and worked is still called the Saddler's Cottage and although enlarged and modernized, the front with an old-fashioned shop-window remains.

There was a Hospital Scheme for which we paid 6d. a week to ensure free treatment. This carried on until the introduction of the National Health Service. The same applied to the District Nursing Service, for which we paid 6d. a month.

The only public house was the King's Head and this is now modernized and more like a restaurant. In 1930 there was one door marked 'Bar' which led into a large room with a brick floor called the Tap Room. Here were played darts, cards, dominoes, etc. Another door marked 'Lounge' led into a much more comfortable room, where the drinks cost more.

There were quite a lot of farm cottages in the village, most of which have been sold. Often two adjoining cottages have been made into one. Others have been enlarged – these have been bought by commuters or retired people from London. It is almost impossible to rent a cottage now. Several new houses and bungalows have been built but most have been too expensive for the local people to buy. Some of the newcomers have entered into the life of the village; they help with the church and the village social activities. One example is the starting of a Carpet Bowls Club in the village hall.

Some women earned quite a lot of money from fruit picking, pea picking or picking up potatoes but today most of the potato and pea crops are harvested by machine and the fruit farmers have either opened their orchards to 'pick your own' or pulled up the bushes and trees, and farm the land as arable land.

In August 1942 I worked part-time on a fruit farm, picking apples and pears but working by the hour, not on piece-work. We had a wage rise of a farthing an hour. On a week of sixteen hours I received an increase of 4d. I also picked blackcurrants once or twice for 2s. for a basket of five pound weight. I was never very good at this and didn't earn very much.

Pebmarsh Church is a large fourteenth-century building. It has three aisles and a large sanctuary. Our rector had written to the Pebmarsh rector in advance of our coming, so we were visited as soon as we arrived. We were taught bell-ringing as there is a peal of eight bells. My husband became a member of the Essex Bell-ringing Association and visited many church towers. I only rang in my own church when they were short of ringers. I wasn't very confident or competent. We also did hand bell-ringing which I enjoyed much more.

Nativity plays were performed around Christmas time. In January 1932 we performed *On the Road to Bethlehem*; in January 1933 we performed *The Saviour's Birth*; and around Christmas and New Year 1934 we played the Yorks Plays of the Nativity. I took the part of the Virgin each time. One year the rector's donkey was walked down to the church for Mary to ride up the church aisle on, but after one rehearsal the idea was dropped as the donkey wasn't very cooperative. These plays were very popular and the church was always full to overflowing. Many people were very sorry when it was decided not to continue with them but the rector's sister was unable to produce any more due to pressure of work and we felt our standard might fall without her professional help. Our last play was in March 1935, when the play *Everyman* was performed in the church. We also performed this in the churches of Castle Hedingham and other local villages. An article appeared in the *Morning Post* on 11 April in which it reported the part of Beauty was taken by an Essex shepherdess. Not strictly true because I only helped my husband – he was the shepherd – although for a long time people called me Mrs Shepherd and it was difficult to get people to stop it.

In January 1932 we were both asked to work for the Church Council as church clerk and sexton, and church cleaner. Every morning the church had to be unlocked and then locked up at night. The first Sunday in the month it had to be open in time for the 7 a.m. service, on Ascension Day for 6.30 a.m. Communion and 7 a.m. on All Feasts Days. From the beginning of October until after Easter two or three tortoise stoves had to be lit on Friday mornings to warm the church for choir practice that evening and kept going until after Sunday evensong. Lighting was by oil lamp and candles. This meant fetching paraffin from the local garage and filling and cleaning more than a dozen lamps and then lighting them whenever lighting was needed. Five large candles had also to be lit. The church had to be swept, dusted and scrubbed. Bells had to be tolled for the evening service, the churchyard kept tidy, and grass cut including round all the graves. The pay for all this was 10s., paid on quarter days.

After one year we decided it was impossible to cope with a large churchyard with so many graves and gravestones. It was impossible to use a lawnmower and it had to be done with a scythe and hand sheers. Considering the church work was in addition to the full-time work as shepherd, we gave up the churchyard work and our pay was reduced by 2s. 6d., leaving us with 7s. 6d. This continued until we resigned in June 1944. No one could be found to take on this work and so my husband was the last church clerk and sexton at Pebmarsh Church.

Being sexton involved digging and filling in graves. Payment for a single six-foot grave was 6s. and 8s. for a double, eight-foot grave. For tolling the bell for funeral services, putting out trestles for coffins to rest on and putting them away again, the sexton received 2s. 6d. As clerk he received 3s. 6d. for putting out services, lighting candles, opening and shutting doors and generally helping the rector before, during and after the funeral.

The death knell involved tolling the church bell twelve or twenty-four hours after a death, every two minutes for one hour. Once for a child, twice for a woman and three times for a man, ending with the continuous number of years of their age. If death occurred after 9 p.m., the bell would be tolled next morning; thus the twelve- or twenty-four-hour rule. The fee for this was 2s. This custom lapsed after our resignation as no one was prepared to do it.

The very large rectory was sold in 1938 and renamed Ralphe Hall after the Sir William Fitz-Ralphe brass in the church. His family held the Manor of the Parish. Ralphe Hall has had a number of owners since 1938 and is now owned by a family making and selling reproduction furniture. The old stables are now workshops. A smaller rectory was built in 1939 and sold in the 1970s. There is now no rector living in Pebmarsh as we are joined with two other parishes and the rector lives in a bungalow in one of them.

In the 1930s there was a lot of social activity in the village. For example, a Men's Club that met in their own building called the Men's Hut. Here they played darts, dominoes, card games of all kinds and held an open Whist Drive on alternate Tuesdays. This closed down in the 1960s. A Women's Social Club held their meetings in the school but closed down in September 1939 and didn't re-open after the war. Men's and Women's branches of the British Legion are still going and well supported. The Flower Show and Garden Society closed down but re-opened as the County Club; this is well supported and holds Summer and Autumn Flower

Shows. A flourishing branch of the Women's Institute carried on until 1986 when it closed down through lack of interest and falling membership. The Mother's Union closed down in the 1950s. Girl Guides, Boy Scouts and the Girls' Friendly Society – all gone a long time ago. The village football team was revived in the 1980s and seems to be going well. The village cricket team survived until fairly recently.

Workers' Educational Association (WEA) courses ended through lack of support, although an effort was made to restart them but not enough people were prepared to attend regularly or pay the necessary fees. As a result they were once again discontinued. Most Saturday evenings there would be some social activity in the village hall. A whist drive and dance, a social with games, handbell-ringing, dancing, lectures, concerts, etc. They were all very popular and well attended. The various organizations would arrange Christmas parties or socials, food, prizes and decorations would be given, and so the cost to the organizers would be very little.

By this time I knew pretty well everyone in the village. I was librarian for many years and secretary and treasurer of the Mother's Union, treasurer of the British Legion for two three-year spells and two spells on the Church Council, and reserve postman, etc. But now I know only a handful of people as houseowners change frequently and house names have been changed. This is the great change in village life compared to the 1930s.

Furrow-drawing and ploughing matches were held in most villages in spring and autumn but much less so now. Many people went for long walks on Sunday afternoons and summer evenings, especially from spring to late autumn. All the footpaths were well-used and kept up. We had a dart board and, in winter especially, friends would come and play darts. We would go to their homes in return.

We had two cinemas in Halstead, three-and-a-half to four miles away. We usually went on Saturday evenings; the first house was at

5.30 p.m., the second house at 8.30, with matinées on Wednesday and Saturday afternoons. The cheapest seats were 6d. and we paid 9d. There were always long queues for the first house. We went on our bicycles because if you went by bus you missed the beginning and end of the film.

In the early 1930s we had gas cycle headlamps. Unless you were very careful and lit them very quickly after turning the water on, the carbide would get too wet and they wouldn't light. We just missed the oil lamp era. No rear light was needed, only a red reflector on the back mudguard – the rear-lamp law came later.

In 1930 transport was not very easy for most people regarding long-distance travel. Although well served with buses for shopping, these didn't run to connect with trains or long-distance coaches. A bus ran to Halstead on Tuesday afternoon and Wednesday to Braintree in the morning, both being market days. Braintree was a long journey through all the villages and didn't return until 4 p.m. Thursdays there was a bus to Sudbury in the morning and afternoon. There were three buses to Halstead on Saturdays and also one for Colchester. Each of these towns had a cattle market but all are now closed. The transport we have now is subsidized by the District and County Council. Travel tokens for pensioners are issued on 1 April. On payment of £8 you received £25-worth of travel on buses, trains and taxis.

In the 1930s, during the summer months, a bus company ran a weekly day-trip service to Felixstowe on Tuesdays and Clacton on Fridays, picking up passengers from the villages. I remember going to Great Yarmouth in Norfolk from Stowmarket in Suffolk with the Silk Works Outing in 1929. This consisted of a convoy of twelve open-topped charabancs – luckily it was a fine, warm day.

I can remember in 1930 seeing turnip seed being broadcast by hand and clover seed by a seed barrow. This was like a wheelbarrow with a wooden bar with spaced holes in it, fixed across the barrow, stretching over the sides by about a yard. I cannot imagine what it must have been like pushing this across the field all day. Charlock was still being pulled out from the corn by hand, and docks and thistles cut off. I still have the old weed hook and other tools that were used by the men in those days. I think it must have been just coming to the end of this work as I don't remember seeing much more after the early 1930s.

The threshing tackle and its team has disappeared almost completely. It was a common sight travelling from farm to farm until combines arrived. It would arrive at the farm with one or two men, who travelled as casual workers and they would sometimes come and ask the farmer for a few days' threshing work. These were the days of the steam engine. After school, boys would come to try to kill the rats as they left the corn stacks. Usually there would be a fox terrier or two enjoying themselves, especially when the bottom of the stack was being reached. Farmers often paid 1d. for a rat's tail to encourage the killing as rats did so much harm, and no warfarin was being used then.

When the corn was cut by horse and binder, men and boys would come and try to catch rabbits as they ran from the corn. It was amazing how they knew when the field was nearly finished. They would arrive running or on bicycles armed with sticks. I have seen many a rabbit killed in this way. Rabbits were prized as cheap food – no myxomatosis in those days. Before the binder started to cut the corn, a band of workmen would scythe a strip wide enough for the horses and binder to travel along without treading on the corn. Now the combine goes straight, cutting the corn before it. Combining was the start of straw burning but after so many complaints there is less of it nowadays. On this farm a straw chopper has been fixed to the combine and all the chopped straw is ploughed back in to the land.

Before combines, many of us would go gleaning. During the cutting by the binder, standing up the sheaves and carting by horse and wagon quite a few ears of corn would be left on the ground. A single sheaf of corn would be left in the middle of the field until the horse rake had been over the field to collect any loose straw and ears. As soon as this was removed anyone could go and glean.

Another custom was the Harvest Supper. The barn would be swept out, seating put in and trestle tables put up. The men would enjoy a good meal and some local entertainment. This is now almost a thing of the past. Harvest Suppers are held but are not connected with farming – simply a means of fund raising.

Farmers went to at least a cattle or corn market each week and almost every town had a corn exchange. One local farmer drove his pony and cart to Halstead each week until he was nearly ninety years of age and then went on the bus for some years, dying at the age of 101!

One custom that has remained longer than most is that bee keepers would tell their bees if there was a death in the family. They believed the bees would die otherwise. I can remember my mother-in-law asking my husband to go and tap on the hives and tell them his father had died suddenly. This was in Suffolk in the late 1930s. Most of these old customs have died out. One no longer heard of is the Rough Band at wedding breakfasts which were never called receptions then. The men and lads would collect old saucepans, frying pans, pails, tins, anything that would make a good noise. They would then go to the bride's home and make as much noise as possible until beer and cake were taken out to them by the bride and groom. I remember my mother making and icing a large cake for them. It was considered almost a disgrace if they boycotted a wedding family party. I am told that in the eighteenth century the opposite was true: this only took place when the wedding was unpopular or considered improper, for some reason.

Children suffering from whooping cough were taken to a flock of sheep early in the morning before the dew had gone. This was supposed to cure them. Alternatively, the child was given a fried mouse to eat. I suppose there were plenty of mice around in those days and they were easily obtained. For a bad cold you had water in which onions had been boiled poured over squares of bread and a piece of butter added. Another thing you could have was two or three drops of eucalyptus on a lump of sugar. For a cough you had blackcurrant tea. This was made by pouring boiling water onto blackcurrant jam that had been made during the summer and kept for this purpose. For a wheezy chest, a tallow or goose-grease poultice would be applied to your chest. Later on Thermogene [medically impregnated sheets of cotton wool] was worn on the chest and back in winter as a prevention rather than a cure. My eldest brother had to endure this as he was considered to be the delicate one. Camphorated oil was another thing applied. I don't know which of these smelt the worst!

I can recall my mother cutting her thumb very badly and when it wouldn't stop bleeding, sending us to the cow-shed to find a large cobweb which she bound round the thumb. Not only did the bleeding stop but it healed very quickly. In these days of antibiotics, people would be horrified. The thing people feared most was tetanus, always called lockjaw then. Everyone knew a person dying from it – always horsemen. The last person I knew was a woman who scratched her hand while gardening. She thought nothing of it at the time but tetanus developed. The local doctors sent a letter to everyone to make sure they were immunized. White linen from old sheets and pillowcases was boiled and stored in airtight tins for use as bandages in emergencies.

CHAPTER EIGHT

DAIRY FARMING IN CHESHIRE

Mrs Emily Owen describes her childhood memories of life on a dairy farm in Cheshire. She is particularly concerned with the work of women on the farm.

I was born on 21 June 1902 at Thornton-in-the-Moors, Chester, where my father was a farmer. Before marriage in 1936 I was a state registered nurse and health visitor. I spent my youth on a big dairy farm in Cheshire at the village of Thornton-in-the-Moors, 7 miles distant from the beautiful city of Chester. It was a rented farm as at that time most land was owned by large estates. My grandfather had been the tenant until my father took over the farm at his death. I well remember the landlady, a widow with a reputation for being a bit of a dragon, called Mrs Park-Yates. Before Christmas she visited the home of each tenant and gave a box of chocolates to the children. Mother, dressed in her best gown, was ready to receive her, no doubt feeling somewhat nervous. The carriage would draw up at the garden gate and the footman, Edwin, dressed in his uniform and with a cockade in his top hat, would race to the front door and announce her arrival. Mother would then proceed down the front path and escort her guest back to the house where she would stay a while for a short chat and take a cup of tea.

Other visitors to the farm were a tinker who called from time to time to repair any leaking pots and pans, and a glazier who carried a heavy wooden frame on his back holding panes of glass to repair the leaded-light windows. He was a huge man with a long black beard and was said to be a Russian Jew. Dark-skinned gypsies, the real Romanies, not today's tinkers, often camped around in their horse-drawn caravans, knocking at the doors selling their home-made pegs and offering to tell your fortune. They would choose a quiet lane with a wide grass verge so they would have plenty of room to draw in and light their camp fire. They would all sit around it, children and adults, talking and cooking whatever they had brought for the pot. They always had a dog or two capable of catching rabbits. Sometimes a big box was slung beneath the caravan housing a few hens. Their horses were tethered around grazing but at night they were often let into a nearby field, of course after dark. It must have been a hard life; they were only allowed by law to stay in one place so long before moving on again.

An Italian woman and her pretty daughter trundled a hurdy-gurdy around the countryside and kept a pair of love-birds in a cage. For $1/2$d. the bird would hop out onto a stick and pick up a small envelope from a little drawer which contained our fortune all written out telling our future.

The postman, Bob, came out from Chester in the morning on his bike and after delivering the letters and daily papers he stayed on all day and helped the farmer who kept the village shop and post office, picking up the evening mail before he returned to Chester at the end of the day. We never wondered where he spent the rest of his life but later I saw him on the doorstep of a small terraced house in town.

We were a big family, six children and our parents with numerous work people around. I remember the whole place was a hive of activity with folk working long hours both inside the house and on the farmyard outside. To stay at a private house bored me to tears; the lack of noise and activity all round was more than I could bear.

Among the livestock on the farm were numerous poultry running free and scratching around for food. Looking for and gathering the eggs was a daily task and full of surprises as they might be laid in the most unlikely places. Also there were ducks on the pond which might take ages to round up in the evening so that they could be safely fastened in to outwit the foxes that were likely to be prowling around. There were sheep for grazing and pigs to use up the whey, the by-product of the cheesemaking. They were housed in sties, brick-built shelters with a walled and paved open run. Most important for the economy of the farm was the herd of around ninety milking cows, which was a big stock for those days. And like many Cheshire producers, the milk was made into cheese which was sold direct to a cheese factor, who called from time to time. Large quantities of water must have been needed and all of this was pumped daily from a pump in the yard which was man-handled as required. In frosty weather the pump looked very exciting with a heavy coat of straw to keep it from freezing. A large coal-fired boiler provided hot water for cleaning and the requirements of the dairy for the cheesemaking process.

Milking, night and morning, was among the main chores of the day. Work began at 5.30 a.m. when all the workers except the horsemen got down to the job. Most women in the village turned out as a matter of course, partly to earn extra money but also it was expected of them as the wives of farm labourers. They collected their milking cans from racks placed in a hollow wall near the dairy. Milking stools were in the shippons which were lit by paraffin-filled hurricane lamps when it was dark. The sound of milk squirting into the empty cans was a magic sound to be remembered. After finishing off each cow the milker emptied his can into a large-sized pail, which stood side by side with its double. When both were full, a lad with a yoke over his shoulders would fasten the chain to each handle, hoist them up and carry them to the dairy where the milk was sieved and emptied into the cheese vat. The head cowman was in charge and responsible for the welfare of the stock in sickness and in health. Shippons, especially in cold weather, were cosy places, very warm with the animals contentedly pulling hay from the cratches and eating cotton cake and chopped turnips out of the stone troughs which ran along the floor in front of them.

Except in the summer, when out in the pasture, the cows were let loose to drink from the pit in the yard, where they would wade up to their bellies in the water – not a very hygienic procedure. In their absence the shippons were mucked out and fresh straw put down for bedding. Each cow knew her own stall and would straight away return to her proper place. The muck was wheeled up planks and tipped from the wheelbarrows onto a huge midden. In the autumn the manure was carted out into the fields and dumped in rucks. Later came the job of muck spreading – it was pitched around the land with a fork.

Feeding stuffs were almost all home-grown: crops of hay, wheat, oats and turnips with potatoes for human consumption. These were stored in huge piles called 'hogs' which meant covering them with layers of straw, then a thick coating of soil to keep out the frost. What hay could not be stored in the bays was built into stacks, sometimes in the field, but preferably in the stackyard. Later the thatcher did his job to protect the contents from the weather. Corn was thrashed and stored in the granary above the shippons, where there was also a huge pigeon loft. At one time the birds had probably been used as a source of fresh meat.

Thrashing was a special event, when the machine arrived with a gang of men. The box was pulled by a steam traction engine. Driving a horse past it in a trap was a hazardous affair – with the animal quite terrified, a man would dash forward to quieten her and lead her past the fearsome contraption.

The railway station being two-and-a-half miles away and the trains inconvenient, we used the horse and trap. Two cobs were always kept for driving, as well as a hunter for my father to ride around the farm and to go hunting on once or twice a week in the season, as did most farmers in those days. With only side lamps lit by a candle on the trap, it was no wonder we were grateful to the moonlight. To make a journey on a pitch dark night, a good deal of horse sense was needed to make the journey safely.

We drove the 7 miles to school in Chester, the girls attending the Queen's School and the boys the King's School. On a cold winter's day it was a chilly experience. One fateful morning the pony slipped and fell on a sticky patch in the street opposite the cattle market. We all took a battering but luckily no one was hurt apart from a few bruises, though Frisky, our pony, had a nasty swelling on her shoulder. We were terrified that anyone at home should find out what had happened and blame us for being careless. To our relief nothing amiss was noticed and we were able to breathe again. So silly of us to be scared when we were blameless.

Three teams of heavy cart-horses and several spares made up the power plant on the farm. The horsemen turned out for work in the early morning, ploughing, sowing and going through the routine work of the seasons. During harvest time all hands on the farm turned out to gather in the crops, working until daylight faded. I remember the magic of walking home from the fields with the evening mist swirling around. Bagging was sent down to the workers – thick slices of bread with wedges of cheese between and plenty of beer to drink to keep them going.

First came the hay harvesting beginning in June. The hay grass was cut by a mowing machine drawn by two horses. After mowing the hay was left to dry, then turned and when ready raked up and piled into cocks. Later it was loaded onto the wagon, lifted up by a hay-fork with a man on top to receive the hay and distribute it evenly to keep the load balanced. This was a skilled job and it was important that this should be done properly to avoid mishaps. The load was then roped to keep it stable and carted up to the farmyard to be stacked or put in hay bales.

Then came the corn harvest: wheat, oats and barley standing high with much longer stalks than today. The heading would be cut by scythe around the field, then the horse-drawn binder was moved in to cut and as it did so, it threw out the binder-twine tied sheaves. These were set up in stooks and left to dry and harden before being carted up to the farm for storing to await the time for threshing. Favourable weather played a vital part in gathering in the crops. A very exciting event was when the area of corn being cut grew smaller and smaller and rabbits began to run out in panic. The guns at the ready blazed away and it was a wonder no one was shot by mistake in the excitement.

Later we celebrated the Harvest Festival. The village church was beautifully decorated with flowers and fruit and corn everywhere, with sheaves tied to the pew ends and spilling out into the aisles. The church was always packed at this special service held on an evening set aside during the week. It was truly a celebration of thanksgiving with all the congregation giving thanks for the blessing received of a harvest safely gathered in.

From time to time several wagon loads of pigs, sheep and calves were taken for sale at Chester Cattle Market. Cattle would be driven on the hoof along the roads and through the city streets till they reached the auction, sometimes out of control, causing panic among the town dwellers.

The men took a great pride in their horses and would come back to the stables in the evening to groom them and bed them down for the night before going along to the village pub for a pint or two of beer.

To help in the extra busy summertime, migrant workers came over from Ireland, leaving their own small crofts in the care of their wives. The same families came year after year and arrived like the swallows in the spring, crossing from Dublin to Liverpool. They were made welcome with a glass of whisky and then they took their few belongings along to the 'shant'. It was a building, one up and one down: very primitive with a trestle table and a few benches, and also a big firegrate on which they cooked their staple diet of bacon and eggs. They were a friendly bunch of fellows except occasionally on a Saturday night, with wages in their pockets, when they would take on an extra load of beer. These Irish 'paddies' were then liable to get out of control and sometimes the result was a good old 'punch-up'. I well remember young Matt, who fell ill and was told by our doctor he had TB [tuberculosis]. My father begged him to go into the local sanatorium for treatment but all he wanted was to go back home to Ireland. By next spring he was dead. Summer over, the Irishmen would depart for home hopefully with a few savings in their pockets including harvest money – no deals for extra pay for overtime in those days.

Work went on apace in the dairy, making cheese and butter. In the house it was cooking and baking bread for the big family of six children and their parents, with four men living in and always two or three girls, with women coming and going from the village to help. We had a plain but good diet. For breakfast, porridge, plenty of bacon and eggs and also cheese melted in the frying pan – cheese was always on tap. For dinner, beef or mutton cut from a huge joint, poultry and stewed rabbit, with plenty of potatoes and vegetables. Rice pudding nearly every day, with pies, stewed fruit and lashings of cream; suet puddings too and jam roly-poly were much favoured. For tea, boiled eggs and bread and butter with home-made jam and cake. There were probably a few luxuries on Sunday, a cream trifle and light cake bought on Saturday from the shop in Chester.

Saturday was very special: it was the day when we had our Saturday penny and we would race off to the village shop to buy sweets. We were always glad when the daughter of the house came through from the kitchen because she was always generous in her helpings from the glass jars, but her mother took the trouble to weigh out each pennyworth of sweets, so we missed out badly and felt very aggrieved when she was on duty.

There was plenty of housework to be done: four fires to be lighted and kept burning, paraffin lamps to be filled and candlesticks to be replenished, and all the cleaning up of a big house, with folk bringing in plenty of dirt from outside. Even the making of the beds was a big undertaking. Most were feather mattresses which needed shaking up and turning each day to keep them the essence of comfort.

On Mondays there were piles of washing that took the women most of the day, working with dolly pegs, dolly tubs and scrubbing brushes. Everything was put through the mangle and if necessary given a boil for extra whiteness and cleanliness. Clothes were then hung out on long lines in the drying ground; should it rain they were put up on big wooden 'maidens' [clothes horses] around the kitchen fire.

Tuesday was ironing with flat irons heated in front of the fire: plenty of starched white linen tablecloths, aprons and pinafores. This was a good day's work, with no mod cons available to make the tasks easier except there were plenty of folk to share the work. No bathroom, no running water, a jug of cold water and a basin on the marble-topped washstand for a quick swill in the morning. We children had a galvanized bath in front of the fire. What happened to the grown-ups is a mystery!

No indoor sanitation, just chamber-pots which were emptied and washed each morning and a privy quite a distance from the house – very matey with a seat for two and overshadowed by a huge sycamore tree. On a dark night it was a case of trooping down the garden *en masse* by the light of a hurricane lamp. With no electricity or gas, a huge kitchen range took care of the cooking. There always seemed to be plenty of hot water from the boiler and roaring fires to keep the house warm. Buying coal by the ton at 6d. per cwt meant fuel costs were not such a problem as today. No electric lights to switch on, only paraffin lamps and candles for light after darkness fell. Reading in bed with a candlestick on the pillow was something of a hazard but we survived. No telephone, so if a doctor was needed it meant a ride of 6 miles to take the message. The same with the fire brigade. When a hay barn was alight, a rider dashing 7 miles to Chester with a request for urgent help brought the brigade tearing along drawn by galloping horses – not much left to salvage by this time, I should imagine!

As children we had complete freedom to roam around the farmyard and the fields. We must have been very sensible and conscious of dangers to avoid; we survived without disaster and there must have been plenty of hazards in the environment. Sometimes we disobeyed the rules and did what was strictly forbidden. We were not cruel youngsters but an event we would not miss was the gory spectacle when a pig was killed for the house. Strangely, we had no inhibitions about eating the delicious pork sausages made a day or so later when the flitches of bacon were laid in the pig turnel [a wooden trough] in the cellar, salted and left until cured ready to hang, when rashers would be cut off with a sharp knife. The tale went that a village lad, not too bright, blew up a pig's bladder to help him to swim in the brook. He made a sad mistake and tied it to his foot. Luckily for him, help was at hand to turn him right side up.

I still have a keepsake to remind me of friends in the village. A very old couple lived near and every Sunday mother sent them dinner and I always helped to carry the tray to their cottage. When they died, within a day or so of each other, I was to have a pair of small figures, a shepherd and a shepherdess, one of their few treasured possessions. Mother too was bequeathed a blue and white plate. All this happened so long ago but it is still as clear in the mind's eye as yesterday. As children we looked upon our farm and its surroundings as the most wonderful place on earth. Memories still are of a happy time when, though life was hard for so many working folk, they were cheerful and contented with their lot. Now all are gone, and even our farm is buried under Shell's industrial complex at Ince and Thornton-in-the-Moors.

CHAPTER NINE

DERBYSHIRE DAYS

This account is based on letters from Mrs Elizabeth Turner and a taped interview by Mrs Jean Skryme to whom I am very grateful for her assistance. Wherever possible I have quoted directly from Mrs Turner's own words. Mrs Turner, née Elizabeth Worsley, was born in Manchester in 1897. Her parents worked in the cotton mills and were sometimes unemployed. She attended a Church of England school and left at the age of thirteen to work in a sweet shop and look after a child. A year later her mother put her name down for a job in the mill, 'but I had to produce my birth certificate to prove that I was fourteen', she remarked. She told me she met her future husband, John (Jack) Turner, in 1922 when she visited the village of Longstone.

I came on a visit on a weekend with a cousin who had been to Longstone during the First World War. She had come with her friends and met my future husband's brother. She started to go about with him and she used to come periodically to see the village, but in those days you weren't allowed to come out without anyone belonging to you, so on this day I came with her for company. There was a 'Wakes' week in Longstone. The field just opposite the cottage where my future husband lived was all laid out by the Wakes people with gingerbread stalls and everything. It was quite amazing. Although Longstone is not that far from Manchester I had never heard of it. I didn't intend to come again but this girl needed someone to go with her, so it fell on me that we both went together.

John's mother came from Rowsley which was then a thriving railway centre. She met his father, a plate layer who lived at Beeley. When they got married they came to live in Longstone because a cottage was available there. John was born there in 1892. He left school at the age of thirteen and went to work on the land. During the War he was in the Army but by 1922 he was back in the village.

We were married in January 1926 and we lived in the second cottage of a row known as Brampton Cottages. The rent we had to pay was 2s. 6d. per week. There were no rates but we had to pay water rates which were 3s. 3d. a quarter. The cottages belonged to the Brampton Brewery Company who owned the White Lion, next to where we lived. Later, another man took over the White Lion and bought the cottages as well. He came from Manchester way. Just before we left it was taken over by a farmer called Cox, who sold the cottages individually.

John had seven brothers and sisters. The eldest was born in Victoria Terrace and when she was about twelve months old they managed to get the other cottage which was two-bedroomed. There were two other families living in the other cottages and they all had six or seven children in those days.

The three cottages had one toilet. You can imagine what it was like. There were always rows because when they wanted to use the toilet they had to go and ask the elderly lady at the end cottage for the key.

In 1922 Jack was working for a farmer called Orrs, but they don't farm now. The other farm still farms today as they have come down from fathers to sons. The only farm in Longstone today is Cox's but when my husband worked there there was Orrs' and Cox's.

In those days there was no electricity and there was no gas, except in some of the big farms. They had big oil lamps to see to do the farm work at night-times when doing the calving or things like that. Gas was just along the main road; there was just an odd gas lamp or two and a man used to go and light them. In the houses you only had the oil lamps, candles in your back part, kitchens and those places. You did everything, including sewing at night, with these. At the vicarage, before my time, it was said the person who used to work there had about forty oil lamps to see to. When you think back you wonder really how the villagers managed but what you don't have you don't miss. You had to do without but we managed. I sewed, I baked, I was used to it.

Here we had a side oven in the cottage and we used coal. I had to get used to cooking on it, and the other side was water. You had to fill it up with water, then you lit your fire: that is where you got your hot water from and then once a year you had to whitewash that out to keep the water clean. We had a big pump at the bottom of the village here which we had to use in the summer-time because there wasn't all these springs. Mind you, there is a good supply of water now but in those days they didn't think that that was there for a purpose. It was one of the ancient rights. Same as the blacksmith's at the bottom here, that was moved when the horses went. We used to go and take the children and watch them put the horses' shoes on – sit there while he did his fire. It was very interesting to watch him.

Down Church Lane there is still a spring which comes down into the troughs by the farm. It comes from the moor. That will dry up at times. The troughs belong to Farmer Cox. There are two big troughs on the side that they fill up and they get water from there. There is one at the bottom of Great Longstone as you turn to go up the moor. There was a trough that used to be there that used to fill up, but this one at the bottom of our yard had to supply you with water during the summer-time because you did get hot summers then. Of course, there weren't water toilets then; only in the big houses. Nobody had a bath indoors; you had a tin bath hung on the wall outside at the back.

Where we lived down the bottom of the 'White Lion', there we had new toilets. Jack said that you used the front of your toilet and the back you threw all your ashes in so they were all mixed together. They were about the newest in Longstone in 1921.

In Manchester, we used ashes but it was sealed off and we had a man come round, a dustman as they called him, to empty them every Monday but they were outside in an entry, as you called it. Everyone had one of these and they used to come and empty them but here you had to empty your own. You'd get somebody to do it, a farmer to take it on the land until such time as he wanted it. There never seemed to be so many diseases around. But in the churchyard there are a lot of children – six months, twelve months old. My husband said there used to be an open sewer went down the village. The sewer beds were down lower here, just off the main road. At the bottom of the village where the last of the houses are on the right-hand side there was a space and the sewerage beds were there.

They had piped water when I came but there was only a certain amount. It would drain off in the summer-time but it was piped into your house. When there wasn't any coming into your house you had to go to the pump and then, of course, it was limey, very limey, but that is why they used to have a big raintub at the back to catch the rain-water. It was the same with the lights. We were the first in the cottages to have electricity laid on but only two lights downstairs – your living room and your kitchen – and in your bedrooms you still had your lamps. When the electricity came it was just for lights because there weren't really many electrical things. Just the bigger people had it. At nights you never went out because there was nothing going on.

When I came here the WI [Women's Institute] had only just started; that was the only thing going in the village apart from the men going to the public houses, playing the darts and dominoes. The women never went out. As I said we used to go to the Women's Institute and there was a choral society with one of the men that came with Longstone Hall – he was the chauffeur, from Manchester. There were one or two people here that had businesses in Manchester. They were big people and they had chauffeurs and gardeners that came with them in the summer-time. There was one of them at Longstone Hall who stayed all along and at the vicarage they had different people at times. I had been in the choir at home so I used to go to that on a Monday night. That was one thing that I was able to go to and the WI but apart from that nothing else until later when another vicar came from Manchester. His wife set up the drama classes then and I used to go down for drama and give these plays. Her daughter today is the head of the Peacock Players but it was started in Longstone and we used to go all over giving plays. There wasn't the people taking up acting then. It was outsiders coming into the village who started things up.

Again it was in the war-time when another family came from Manchester. They came to work for Mr Thornhill the poultry man and we started the British Legion Women's Section. Lady Stephenson became our president. I was the chairman and she was the secretary and we ran the Legion for the women. We had a big section of it then and I was the one that got the first Derbyshire Gold Badge for the British Legion. I was chairman for ten years. We raised the most money for it. It was mostly the men who had been in the War that joined the Legion. Usually your husband or brothers had been in it. My husband had been a member of the Legion from 1919 and, of course, there wasn't a Women's Section here. Acle had had a Women's Section before we started in Longstone. We did a lot of work and raised a lot of money for it. I was ill and was giving up and getting someone else to come and take it with no idea that they were going to give me a present from the headquarters, and I have the gold brooch here now. You cannot buy them and if you lost it you couldn't have another one. It was in the papers then. I had a photograph in the *Derbyshire Times*, in those times, with Lady Stephenson pinning this gold badge, which I knew nothing at all about. I always used to wear it and especially if we went out. I wore it when I went on processions in London with the Legion and to the conferences at London. We used to go once a year. I used to go and the secretary or president would go.

In the summer-time we started having fêtes with roundabouts and various 'Queens' and we started all this business which got the village going more then, you see. There were more houses being built, council houses. Some of the people were coming from other villages into Longstone. Some were coming from Ashford. They were working at the marble works and coming to live at Longstone because they were building houses in the village and not at Ashford. Then, of course, a lot of people started coming when Thornhill started his poultry. They started coming from Broseley. In those days the girls came on bicycles.

The poultry business was going before the War but only in a very small way. You could count on your fingers the people who worked there. The chickens were all bred here to begin with. Then they had egg packing during the War. They got more fowls, you see, and then the dried egg was put on the market.

When I first came here I was travelling by train. I used to go home at least once a month and going on the early trains there was Mr Stephenson – he was made a baronet during the War. He used to come in his car with his chauffeur to Longstone Station to go in this train in the morning to Manchester. People used to use the trains. They used to come out weekends for hiking – we call them Ramblers today – and the trains used to be full of people at week-ends. That is why it was such a shock when they took the trains off. Monsal Dale was always a place for people coming to the dales. In those days the train service was very popular. It was Beeching that finished that. We fought for it from the Legion; we all went down, and there was Thornhills, Wrights the solicitors. We all went down to either Derby or Nottingham where they had the big meeting. We all travelled by the railway just to show them. I know even then it had all been settled by Beeching and the big people. I had to speak as I was a Manchester person why we wanted the trains kept on. When we sat down I sat next to Mr Wright and I said, 'I don't think we have a dog's chance of keeping our trains.' He said, 'I don't think we have.' I said, 'I think it is all settled.' And it was! So that was how our train service went. Then they said they would put buses on for us, which they never did. I think that was one of the reasons why my husband decided he wasn't going to stop here. But then he had to come back – it was through me. The funniest thing was I was blamed for him leaving Longstone; I was taking him from his birthplace to Cleveleys, Blackpool, and it didn't suit him and he had to come back to the moors again.

I lived in Blackpool for two-and-a-half years. I had to stop there. I couldn't go out near the sea. We were so near the sea but higher up than Blackpool we were, near Cleveleys, and, of course, it was only like going to the end of where the cottages are here but we were close on the sea and it was the sea air. I couldn't make out why I couldn't get my breath because we had stayed year after year. I had been there during that year and I had been ill. I was took ill as I came back but our doctor he could have said he didn't know whether it would suit me. I suppose he never thought of it. The doctor they had to bring to me – you see I couldn't breathe – as soon as he examined me, he turned to my husband and said, 'Well, you can't stay here', like that. We sold up and everything. The doctor said, 'You've had a viral pneumonia', which we didn't know. In those days we would have said double pneumonia, we didn't know there was a difference. Of course, it was then they brought out the antibiotics. It was funny that, because Molly Thornett, she got it. She went all over the big places to try and get it for the doctors because it hadn't come through. I forget what it was called but they said it was only that that could save a life. It was only then that the doctor could tell us that the left lung was damaged and that was why I couldn't stop there. All those years from being well in my teens, it was nearer to go from Manchester for holidays.

I was pleased to come back here, because they said it was my best plan to get back to the moorland air and I thought if we went anywhere else, we didn't know whether it would suit us. We answered this questionnaire which they sent round to say if they were building any old people's places, were we in favour? Of course, we said 'Yes' and it was through that that we got back here. It had to be didn't it? We were lucky.

There weren't a great lot of children going to school when I came. The only thing was as they got work they left the village: the girls went into service and the youths got village work, you know, as farm labourers and that. It was not until I had been here for about twelve months they opened a factory in Bakewell and one or two of the girls then that were leaving school got taken on. It was called the Granby Garment Company, I think, and they used to make knitted things. They got work in that place until Bakewell began to grow with big factories, so that kept a lot of them in the village what had had to go out before into the big houses and take jobs.

After the First World War, the Rural Council was then looking after the roads. So they used to take a man on for rural council work, digging because they were muddy roads and they used to empty the stone onto the roads and then level it out. That was all that was done when I first came and there was just one man then that used to see to them. From that time, my husband was still farming. The County Council had taken over from the Rural Council and started putting the roads in order; that was in 1926–7. When I had been here a while with my husband, farming started to go down and one or two of them looked for other jobs. So my husband was taken on with the Derbyshire County Council. This would be around 1930. He worked as a roadman, hedging, ditching and patching the roads. The surveyor lived in the village and sometimes called Jack out late at night to help clear snow or grit the roads.

When I first came, there wasn't a great lot of the children going to school but they had quite a good education here. There was a headmaster and one or two teachers, all at one school. They didn't have the different subjects that we had in Manchester but they were quite good with the education. Some of them, my age, had gone away from the village so there was just the others that were growing up. It was a Church of England school and still is and the children always had a church service in the mornings in the school before they started their lessons. The minister used to go in once a week to give a scripture lesson to them and on all the different saints days they all went to church and kept all the other holy days up. The children had concerts and such.

When we were first married, my husband and I had to bring up the remainder of the family, as both his parents were dead and his brother had married the girl I came with from Manchester, and had left home. We did this on £2 a week, including working all day on Sundays. Eventually we were left with the youngest girl, who was only twelve. She carried on at Longstone School with us looking after her. She joined in everything, including church, and that was the beginning of how I got on in the village. Because I had been superintendent of the Sunday school in Manchester and in the choir, the vicar there sent all particulars to the vicar of Longstone. Then I was welcomed with open arms into everything.

In the villages in those days you weren't considered one of them until you had been there for quite a while. To begin with, often they were very bitter because they were all inter-married – Ashford people, Longstone people, Little Longstone people and other local village people. It was only after the First World War that one or two people began to come out here with the railway. Signalmen were sent out from Manchester way and they got married and got cottages.

John's father died in 1921 during the 'flu epidemic and his mother died in 1922. She wasn't very strong after the father died. For the funerals in those days, they all walked with the coffin on the bier and all the village followed. There was no hearse and the undertaker was the builder that lived at the side of our house on the main road. Mr Ayres, his name was, and they did the building and ng and everything. It seemed very funny to me. The first time anybody died I saw the coffin brought up on one of the builder's lorries. They were laid out in the houses in those days and then from there, this Mr Ayres who did the undertaking part, just walked in front of the bier and all the villagers walked behind up to the church with the vicar or the chapel people. They only had to come down the main road and go up the main street. In those days that was how that was conducted.

We always kept Remembrance Day at the school and we used to stop all the traffic at 11 o'clock right on the very day – not just the Sunday, as we have it now. It was always 11 November at 11 o'clock. They used to bring the children from the school down onto the main road and they used to stand us all in the yard. When I first came the people in the village always used to walk up and commemorate it with the children. Then we managed to get a cenotaph. There were quite a lot of people from Longstone killed in both wars.

There were the Odd Fellows and the Buffaloes Friendly Societies in the village, and on the Odd Fellows Day, they went to church with a beautiful big, silk banner and the men had different things they wore. They used to have a day off work, fitting in different hours to get the milking in and that. They had a service at the church, then they used to come to the White Lion and have a dinner. Just for men, no women were allowed in public places. Then, at dinner-time they would go back to their own business and at night the wives or young ladies were allowed in the back of the White Lion. There was a bar where they could entertain. There was a youth in the village that played a fiddle and we used to dance to the fiddle.

Most of the men belonged to a Friendly Society and they were just for the men. If you lived in the village or about you could join, because my husband said, when he was a youth the fathers always put the sons in at fourteen in the Odd Fellows. It was a sort of insurance and they could draw it when they were sick, and I think the doctor used to come out to these people, to certify that they were ill. Then there was the Buffaloes: that was started in Ashford to begin with and then some of the Ashford men working in Longstone brought the Buffaloes to Longstone. And the Longstone men joined the Buffaloes as well and they used to give a party for the children at Christmas.

There was no village doctor, we had the Bakewell doctors. In those days there were two doctors in Bakewell. When I first came there was a Dr Fenton and Dr Jackson and then there was another one, a Dr Evans. If you wanted a doctor in a hurry, someone had to go to Bakewell to get one. Today we have 'phones. During wartime we had a doctor came in the village and this is what makes us all cross. Our doctor had a surgery in the village on a Friday and on a Wednesday, in a house near the White Lion. Later he had that fitted up so you could go there on a Tuesday night or on a Friday night. He mixed his own drugs because his wife was a pharmacist. Today even when the doctor has been or the sister, she doesn't do it, you have to send your prescription into Bakewell to get your drugs. So it means if there is nobody going to Bakewell you have to pay somebody to go for you on the bus and get it for you. It seems funny today that everything is worse. My doctor is very good and as soon as we 'phone, if he is there, he will come out if it is something he knows, and the same with the sister.

There was a village lady who 'laid out' people and I've done it myself. I had helped my mother who went out sick nursing in Manchester and I got to know a lot about sickness. They used to come for my mother then in Manchester and say, 'Mrs Worsley, can you come? My Dad has passed away and me mother says can you come.' Of course, I didn't know what it was for at one time. I don't know how it came about, there was no one to help my mother so she said to me, 'Can you come? It will stand you some good', not that I was any of an age. A lady had died and my mother told me what we had to do. I had to straighten the limbs out and, of course, I did all she told me to do. Then she said, 'That is alright now for the doctor to see', and from then it seemed to grow with me. When I came here – I don't know whether Jack had said it to anybody – but this person come up that night, it was on a Saturday night and very dark, 'cos I tell you I hadn't any light. She said, 'Would it be possible if Mrs Turner could go and help her to lay this man out?' I looked at Jack and he said, 'Come in.' She said, 'I've always had someone to help me and the other person that helped me has moved and nobody else seems to want to help me and I cannot do it on my own. So Jack said you would help me, as you had done it with your mother.' So that is how I got let in with her. I did it with her quite a few times. When you look back, I thought why was I sent here to do them things? I did them and I got through with them. Then they started having a district nurse in the village, so she used to see to people doing these jobs. I sat up many and many a night with people expecting their babies and everything seemed to go alright. We were all there in the cottages to help one another.

You mixed in and did what you could do. They knew what you could do and they relied on you. Then, of course, as I said, the village grew bigger after the war-time and we had plenty of people coming in the villages, like holiday people. And, of course, when the War was on, two of us did the catering, for when the evacuees came. We had the institute with a great big old boiler that we had to scrub out, and make soup for all these people coming from London. Of course, the trains were useful, you know, to Longstone. And the evacuees, one lot from Manchester and one lot from London we had. We had the institute to feed them in but a lot of them didn't stop, a lot went back. At Longstone Hall, the people living there were Plowrights. They were Sheffield steel people, I think, and they were the only big people in the village that took a lot of children in. The others would take a teacher but not children. The cottages in Longstone were taking two or three children in but when they went to ask the others if they could billet perhaps a girl or boy, 'Oh no. Have you got a teacher? We'll have her.' Mr Plowright had his top storey at Longstone Hall made into a great big room, a dormitory for about eighteen to twenty girls – high school girls, some school from down London way. Those girls stayed in the village right up to the end of the War before leaving and those girls were a great asset to the village. They helped in the Sunday school with the children and things like that. But all the others – Oh, my word! A lot of the people from Manchester way, they more or less went back.

John had worked on the land since he'd been thirteen, from a boy he had been on the farm helping, and he was on the farm till two years after we were married. Then they decided to do it themselves and he got a job at the quarry then. There were no jobs available to get and this farmer stopped the two of them and another farmer also stopped the two that worked for him as they were doing the work themselves. Jack was very lucky. He went to this builder who was living next to where we lived. Mr Ayres had known Jack from being young but he had no chance of setting anybody on. He had enough men of his own so he sent him to Bakewell and that was when he came to know about the Rural Council. They sent him to the man who was over the surveyor and he didn't want any at the time, but he asked my husband if he knew this man at Ashford who was running this quarry down at Monsal Dale for the Rural Council. Jack knew him, so he said, 'If he can offer you a job, tell him to start you.' When he went, he was told there was a man leaving in a fortnight and he could have his job. So, right away he wasn't out of work long. Soon he was working at Monsale Dale Quarry, right at the bottom of the dale. He had never been used to quarry work but he took it on and also got this other chap that had been stopped from farming. I suppose he thought he had been used to outdoor work.

The farmers, they were doing it themselves, as they weren't very well off so they were cutting the farms down. So there was no outlook. You could only get odd jobs outdoors you know, but Jack was very lucky. He went straightaway that very night they told him, to that builder and from there to Bakewell. The same night he went walking as there was no transport from Bakewell to Ashford.

On the farm, his regular job started about seven in the morning till any time at night. They had to be there for the milking but did have time off to come home for lunch from the farm in the village, and in the morning, he came home for his breakfast, which he came for after he had done the milking. He had to take the milk to Longstone Station to catch the milk train. There was a whole row of ponies and carts and that, from Ashford had to come to Longstone Station and you could hear the rattle of all these carts going down Station Road. If you were going by that train you could see it coming along from Bakewell and you would be hurrying up to get there because you knew they had to load these 'milk kits' as I got used to calling them. So every morning it was the same people saw one another. It was very interesting to me to begin with. It was lonely in one sense because I lost all the companionship I had been used to but it was a different outlook, although at times it was very lonely, like I am now. At night-time we waited for Jack coming in after he had bedded the cattle down in winter and that. They milked twice a day, morning and night – out of doors in the summer in the fields, as far as Monsal Head they had fields. They used to go and sit with a little three-cornered stool, you know, and many time a thunder shower started when they had begun milking and they had to carry on. The milk went into small cans when they were milking under the cow and then they emptied them into big churns. The milk went straight from the cow into the churn and then down to the train. The milk then went to places like Manchester.

When I had lived in Manchester there wasn't a lot of fresh milk delivered. There was the condensed milk. People took tea and sugar with them to work. Together with the condensed milk we tipped in boiling water. My father used to have to take his like that to work but we were able to come home because we weren't very far from work and mother was at home. The only thing we used to take was our breakfast with us as we only had half an hour for breakfast. It was from 8.30–9.00 a.m., our breakfast. We started at 6 o'clock and then we used to come home at 1 o'clock till two – we had an hour's break in the mills. We had time to go home for our break but lots of the mill people didn't go home for their meals; they just took it in baskets or cans or anything – sandwiches you see. From then we had to work until half past five, we didn't get any other break.

Milk wasn't bottled. I can remember in some of the shops they had great big white mugs, as you would call them, and on them it used to have MILK in black letters and they would tip milk into there and cover it up. People used to go in and they used to measure it out with cans into their utensils. The old people used to say, 'Will you bring me ¹/₂d. worth of milk from so-and-so's?'

In winter the cows' feed was all chopped up. Turnips, there was black treacle and turnips, all chopped and put through a mangle in the big places where the cows were. The farmers grew the green stuffs and the turnips and potatoes on the farm. When I first came I was surprised to see treacle given to cows as in Manchester we used to eat a lot of black treacle on bread. So when Jack brought a tin of black treacle home that the boss had given him, as he had heard a lot of people ate this, I told him it was the same as what we used to eat and he said, 'Of course it is.' I said, 'Why do you give it to cows?' Whether it was a regulation to give it to cows I don't know.

It was a mixed farm but no free milk or anything like that. The only milk they didn't sell was the first milk after calving. They used to use it for themselves and any of them that worked for them got it – 'beastings' it was called. Jack used to take a big can with him when a cow or two cows calved and he said, 'I will be bringing some home so you can make some custard with it.' We used to make lovely thick custard with it; you didn't put no egg or anything with it, only sugar. So that was the only thing we ever got. We laughed I can tell you, about one thing, when we were getting married at Manchester. It was after Christmas time, 23 January, when Jack came he said they had given him £2 to get a wedding present which, of course, was a lot of money in those days. So I thought we were going on our honeymoon to his sister's at Croydon so we will take this £2 separate and perhaps there would be something we would see to buy with it. I forget what it was but we took it with us and we bought something with it. We were down there a week and then we came home and spent another weekend with mother and Mark before I came to Longstone. The snow was laying and we had had no snow in Manchester. He was having to go to work the next day but this was Sunday and he was going on Monday, so he says, 'I should think they will give me a week's wage', but did they? No! The £2 for his wedding present was his week's wages and we had spent it on a present. So looking back on those days it was no good grumbling – you just had to accept it.

We never had anything to save because we were bringing his sister up, a lovely girl but we didn't get anything for her in those days. But his sister at Croydon, her husband was badly knocked about in the First World War, they managed to get a little delicatessen place because his grandfather was an alderman at Croydon then, and he managed to get this little shop affair for him and fitted it out. Her husband's face one side was all cut away including the eye and everything. He was a good scholar and he used to have groceries and deliveries to people round about them. There was a lot of people around Croydon in them days and she used to cook because she had been a cook at one of the big houses here and then she had moved to Manchester. She had worked in the YMCA [Young Men's Christian Association] during the First World War at Manchester so she was a good cook. In those days she was doing rissoles and those things that they do today; she was selling them out there and that is how they first started.

When she got a piece of bacon and perhaps one end was a bit fatty – people said they didn't want any fat – she would cut a lump off that and send it up to me. I used to cook it as it helped to make us meals with Sarah being there. The same with sewing, my sister could always sew. Lily her name was. When Sarah was being confirmed at thirteen at church, I said to my sister, could she get something cheap that I could manage to do some sewing with, because she couldn't keep coming over. I remember it was that broderie anglaise and I made her a confirmation frock after my sister sent some of that. I did the top and it looked like some you see today. I sewed it by candlelight because I was a good hand-sewer. I always used to finish my sister's hand-sewing off when she was making frocks for us. You look right back and I think many a time how we used to read; we read at night, books and that, and yet today you wouldn't. Would you not with a candle on the table? So it must have altered our eyesight then, you know, the light, because as I said we only had candles. We did have a big lamp and people used to come and look at it because that was a wedding present to us. It was a big wedding present from some lady and Jack used to polish this brass bowl and fill it you know, because I had no dealing with lamp oil, as it was called. We used to have that lit when we were doing anything. Other times we used to sit with a candle on a table – and in the kitchen to wash up and do your cooking you had in the winter-time, a candle.

I say, through altering the clocks, things have altered completely because there was no clock altering then. We used to sit outside those cottages. We sat outside with Mrs Parker next door, and we had a garden same as was round the front, as well as the garden where we had vegetables and we used to grow flowers. We would sit there and she would be knitting and I would be knitting, I'd be stitching and she would be stitching. She had three boys and a girl and she was doing all this and her husband was a farm labourer. He worked at Hassop because his mother was a widow and she had two sons like Jack's age; they worked for the mother and that was one of the Hassop farms that they lived at. But Mr Parker used to come home every night and he used to go the same time as Jack next morning. Especially at hay time we would look at one another about 12 o'clock and say to one another, 'About time they were coming, you know.' And you would hear the farm boots coming up and she would say, 'Here they both are, coming home together.' They used to set out together, one going to Hassop and my husband going to Longstone, but it was a regular occurrence that, you see.

The haymaking was all done by hand. The hay was turned with the forks and that, and loaded onto the hay drays. The men stood up there forking it on and pressing it down. I remember corn time; it was always stooking up the sheaves of corn in the fields, far different from today. That was a big thing to me because I had never seen that in Manchester.

The Irishmen came all through the summer. They stayed the whole of the summer. They came at haymaking time and the first hay was cut 24 June, I always remember that. And the Irishmen would come either the week before that or the weekend ready for starting and they stayed till everything was gathered in – I don't mean all the other harvesting, just the hay and that, and they would stay all of the time. It was funny, I remember, it was year after year the same men that used to come all the way. They were nice Irishmen and the farmers used to put them up in these great barns – they were like dormitories. They used to have their meals at the farms, you know, and go in the pub at night with the men. Yes, it was a jolly time. The village was alive when they were all here, you know. You mixed about more but as I said many a time, there was nothing going on until after the second war.

The wives didn't help very much with the farm work – they never went into the farm. The farmers had their own domestic people: they would have perhaps a couple of cooks and women doing the cleaning and that, or day-women going in but the farmer's wife did a lot. You never saw anybody else in the farms, only their own people and their own workers.

Jack used to have a big patch outside to grow our own vegetables and during the Blitz on Manchester, my sister came and she used to go down with Jack, as we had another allotment then, down at this other village, and she used to go down with him and she used to help him and she used to do all the garden at the back, the vegetable garden. She even helped with the garden here; even when Jack died she would say, 'Jack would be putting such a thing in now, I had better get some. Get some money and the next time you are in Bakewell get them.' She was taken, and I am left and I am no good with gardening at all to tell you the truth. But when we first married we had to rely on home-grown vegetables.

There were four shops in the village: one was the post office, another was the grocer, something like the Co-op, a big shop nearly opposite the White Lion. There was a man and a youth used to serve in there. Then just a bit higher up, there was a house that sold everything from leather bootlaces to anything. It was always open and it was there for years and years but, of course, it is pulled down now and another bigger shop is there now. There were about four, that is all. I forgot, there was one butcher and there is still about the same there today. One shop has finished and they have made a house of it. As you go up the village towards Monsal Head, that used to be where they baked and did seed cakes and bread. We used to make our own bread in those days. The first thing on Monday morning when Jack used to go to work and Sarah went to school, I used to mix half a stone of flour, that would be rising while I was doing the washing. My mother came over to stay and she went to Bakewell and bought a paraffin stove with two burners and a tin bath to put on top. I boiled my whites this way for about five years. In Manchester I had used a copper built into the house and was at a bit of a loss in Brampton Cottages, so I copied my neighbour, Mrs Parker, who had beautiful whites. She boiled the washing in batches in the oven, after cooking Sunday dinner, drying it outside on Mondays.

One day I went with my mother to the Co-op in Manchester where I saw lots of coppers all fitted for use with gas. The Co-op had a system where they gave you a ticket to take to your local Co-op who would then get the goods required. However, I could not make the Bakewell branch of the Co-op understand that I needed a copper without the gas connection. Anyway a local ironmonger provided me with a copper, cut out the gas pipes and fitted a small primus stove in their place. I used this for a number of years.

I spent some time in the early days trying to make bread, wash and iron on the same day, but after my mother had stayed here she told me to leave the ironing until Tuesdays. Later bread was baked at Ashford and there was also a horse-drawn bread cart which supplied the villages over a wide area. Quite often it arrived in Longstone during the early evening.

One thing I was surprised to find, how people were so looked after by charities. First was the Holme Meal Charity, which was flour given to the poor families which had to be brought in a pillow-case and used for baking bread. Another was the Wright Charity and on a New Year's morning you would see sons armed with two baskets, one with pieces of beef and the other with cobs of bread. I remember another was a gift of flannel which my young sister-in-law had to go to the vicarage to receive as the mother was very ill.'

CHAPTER TEN

HARD TIMES IN SUFFOLK

Mrs I. W. Pearson's account points out the harsh conditions of country life in Suffolk in the early years of the twentieth century.

I was born in London and went to Wrentham in Southwold in Suffolk when I was a little girl. There was an acute shortage of houses even then and our family considered themselves very lucky to get a property suitable to house ourselves, various elderly relations, together with cats, dogs, rabbits, chickens and pet white rats! The property was part Georgian, part Victorian and was Church property. The house consisted of a large hall and rooms downstairs, and upstairs the bedrooms ran into one another. They were kept warm by the bread-oven flue and the kitchen range, though the cooking was done by a blue flame Valor oil stove. The sanitary arrangements consisted of an outside earth lavatory. No water apart from two deep wells. The rent was 10s. per week, rates £2 10s. per half year, collected by the rates officer with a pony and trap. Tithes paid to the Church yearly, a rose a year for the renting of a piece of land near the property for vegetable growing.

There was a cottage adjoining, where two elderly sisters lived who we took under our wing. And two other cottages, one occupied by a land worker and his family, the other by an old gentleman who declared, 'God didn't pay rent', and he wasn't going to!

Rather surprisingly the farm worker in the other cottage had a small library of books written by the Russian revolutionaries of the time. The only member of the family that could read, read aloud after tea. I should think the idea of reading aloud these books after a day pulling up frozen beets from wet fields must have been rather hard work.

There was the usual religious views, fighting each other from chapels and the two churches. My family went to them all in turn. The village had a chemist, four village shops, two linen drapers, two bakers, a cheesemaker, basketmaker, a wheelwright and black-smith and a boot-mender; also two dressmakers, a greengrocer, a post office and a branch of a bank which opened one day a week for three hours. Also there were two carpenters, a carrier, two butchers, a doctor, a district nurse and a vet. There were four pub-lic houses, a garage and one public telephone. There was a mole catcher who made wonderful mushroom ketchup; also a road-mender, miller and postie.

The average wage for the shore fisherman was £100 per year but the shops all made a living – I don't know how. The threat of going to the Parish Relief hung over many; it was considered a deep dis-grace. The workhouse was the fate in store for some of the old people, although many muddled through with help from here and there. The church was beautiful, always well attended but I cannot remember it doing much for the people, only collecting tithes due which annoyed the local farmers. Women still collected stones from the fields for 1d. a bushel basket and went faggoting after a storm for their fuel. There were plenty of children who survived measles, whooping cough and the summer ailments very well on the whole.

The village hall was a gift to the village from the local squire on the understanding there was no drinking and everything finished by 10 p.m. There, pictures were shown once a week, with a break in the middle while the last part of the film was fetched over by motorbike from Southwold. The village concerts were always held there and the local whist drives. The best entertainment was a monthly meeting of the village councillors at which my grandfather and the village dominie [parson] had a blazing row which carried on at every meeting. The village library and reading room was furnished with beautifully bound copies of various sermons by, no doubt, very clever scholars. There was also the *Boys' Own Magazine* which I loved, provided by the squire, I believe, and various ladies magazines of the Victorian era.

The real strength was in the schools and their wonderful teachers, who were ill-paid, yet taught children from three to fourteen years, ignoring the squeak of lead pencils on slates, cold, chilblains and the smell of wet rags used for cleaning slates and blackboard, and also of children that had one bath a week, if they were lucky, earth closets, and having to change the children's wet clothes after long walks to school. Luckily they could always rely on my grandmother's supply of dry clothes which she made out of old clothes donated by the more affluent members of the village. There was a chronic lack of employment over the countryside and for the women it was very difficult. It was domestic work or work on the farm for the older women, while for the young girls it meant going to the cities as servants, which sometimes resulted in loneliness and overwork.

The old folk could only look forward to the workhouse or a miserable life in a damp, cold cottage, living on what the Parish Relief handed out. It was so bad one winter, we organized a soup kitchen – soup made from gifts of vegetables, meat, game, anything my grandfather could beg from the farms and shops. It was 1d. a pint, old folk a milk-can free, delivered by me. I must have been the first 'meals on wheels' or on foot. We were on the direct route to the Blythburgh Workhouse and if they didn't make it by nightfall, they spent the night anywhere, in the barns or sheds. One old man froze to death in our garden.

The steam machines had at that time taken over, although there were quite a few ploughing horses, and the shepherds used movable huts like bathing machines, and the hedgers and ditchers were moving about. The Army took many of the young men away from the farms who were just fed up with low wages, primitive housing conditions, lack of clean water and with a future that offered only hard work and very little pleasure.

CHAPTER ELEVEN

POTATO PICKING
– THE FLYING FIVE

Potatoes have been a major crop in the Fen district of Cambridgeshire for many years. As they are a seasonal crop most farmers employ casual workers to harvest the crop, and much of the work has always been done by women. The work is often organized by gang masters who employ the women and hire them out to local farmers. Today they usually arrange to transport the women from their homes to the farm on which they are working.

However, in the years before the First World War there was at least one group of young women in the March district who organized themselves into a gang and cycled to work on the farms. I was told about this group by Mrs C. Betts, a grand niece of one of the original members of the group. She also supplied copies of photographs taken by a *Daily Mirror* photographer. The group was known locally as The Flying Five, though there are seven or eight girls shown in most of the photographs.

Potato picking was a hard strenuous job. At that time many farmers were still using an adapted plough to turn up the potatoes, though some would have been using the potato lifter, which consisted of a share that passed under the potatoes which were lifted out of the ground by tines. This was a relatively light machine pulled by a single horse. Other farmers might have been using the

On the way to work. A gang of girls going potato picking

Arriving at work. The girls park their bicycles at the side of the field

150

Jumping the dyke. In the fens the fields are often divided by dykes rather than fences

Picking the potatoes

Bagging up potatoes. Here the potatoes are being put into bags for immediate use rather than being stored in clamps

potato spinner in which the tines revolved to spin the potatoes out of the ground. This was a heavier machine that had to be pulled by two horses. These machines were driven by a horseman.

The potatoes were then picked up by women carrying large willow baskets. When the baskets were full they were emptied into a cart which took them to the end of the field where a clamp had been prepared.

Before the potato lifting started, a space near the field gate was levelled and covered with a thick layer of straw. On this the potatoes were piled. The clamps would be about two yards wide at the base, tapering to a point at the top, and from fifty to a hundred yards long, depending on the number of potatoes to be stored. After the potatoes were laid out and piled up they were covered with straw to keep them dry and to prevent the soil from getting mixed with the potatoes. Then the straw was covered with a layer of soil about one foot thick to protect the potatoes from the frost in the winter. Every two yards along the top of the clamp, a straw 'dolly' was put in to allow any heat from the potatoes to escape.

The potatoes were stored in the clamps until they were needed to send to the market. Then they were riddled and sorted, again usually by the women. The best potatoes would go to the market to be used for human consumption, and inferior or small potatoes would be used to feed pigs or other animals.

CHAPTER TWELVE

FROM SHROPSHIRE TO DERBYSHIRE

Miss Rosetta Bell tells of her youth spent in Shropshire and Derbyshire.

I lived in Shropshire as a child. I remember the First World War, seeing the Zeppelin passing over Market Drayton and seeing coloured soldiers in uniform passing by. Living in the country you did not see a lot.

We were a large family; my mother had five boys and five girls. We lived on a smallholding with a number of cows, sheep, pigs, ducks, geese and turkeys. But these were not enough to support our large family, so my father worked on a farm nearby, often for as little as £1 10s. a week, starting work at 6 a.m. and returning home at 6 p.m. with one hour off for his dinner. My eldest brother used to go to the farm with my father and help him at 6 a.m. He milked ten cows and cleaned out the pigs. My next eldest brother brought the cows up out of the field, while they were cleaning out the troughs and putting the corn out ready for the cows to eat – they let the milk down better if they are eating. So my brother was late for school on many occasions.

Being late for school, even though he was often only five minutes late, he always got the cane. Many children got the cane for lateness when they had been out at 4 a.m. picking potatoes. We also got the cane if we did not curtsy or the boys forgot to touch their caps to the parson, people who lived at the hall or other people of importance.

When my brothers left school, they found work on the farm at 5s. per week, live-in and half day off a week. They gave their money to my mother to help bring us up. As one by one we left school, we left home and sent our money home, till in the end we bought our own farm.

My mother used to bake forty loaves a week. We had oat cakes for breakfast and she used to buy 1 cwt of flour, 1 cwt of oatmeal, and 1 cwt of wheatmeal. We grew our vegetables and we had a potato hog [for storing potatoes] and turnips for the winter. She was a good woman and we were all brought up to attend a place of worship. I never married and cared for her until she was ninety-four years of age. I looked after things at home – everyone's odd person.

My brother rode a bike, from Shropshire to Cheshire, to look for work. Often the farmer used to ask to see his hands. If they were clean he didn't get the job because they didn't look like working hands. But my brother also looked at their dog and if it was thin he would not go there because he said, 'If they cannot feed their dog, they could not feed me properly!' – he loved his food. Often my brothers went as far as fifty-five miles to look for work and answer adverts for, 'Men wanted for farm work'. When they got there they were told the post was filled – not even got a cup of tea. They then rode back on their bikes the fifty-five miles.

We used to kill a pig now and again. We were poor but I never knew what it was to want food – we were very careful. My father was too poor to drink and worked so hard that when night-time came he was too tired to go out, but he was nearly seventy-five when he passed on with a stroke.

We left Shropshire in 1933 and came to a hill-country farm at Rowarth, Derbyshire, in 1933. All the cows and sheep we had brought with us died after leaving the rich luscious grass of

Shropshire. We came to a poor barren farm that had never been ploughed – everything died. So we started all over again, all pulling our weight.

Often the snow was 20 foot in the winter. We had to dig the sheep out and the hen-cotes. An old man lived in the next farm with his wife who was ill. The man made a cup of tea from the snow outside the door – his wife died. We saw a flag blowing on the chimney and on investigation we found he was ill as well. The snow was a yard deep. He wore straw in his clogs but no stockings. Unfortunately he died. My brother-in-law took ill, he fell and had a strangulated hernia. He managed to walk doubled up over three fields to our farm, for me to come and care for his three children, as his wife was in hospital having her fourth child. I had two-and-a-half miles' walk to the doctor's but he did not come because the snow was too deep. I went again next day while my mother looked after the children and I told the doctor's wife I had come in the deep snow and he could come also. Before I got back he had been and was ordering the ambulance. My brother-in-law was called the 'miracle man' in Stockport Infirmary. He had pain every breath. After three months he came home. I stayed there six weeks to help them.

We were very near the highest point of the Pennine range – Kinder Scout. We walked four-and-a-half miles to sell eggs. Everyone was doing the same. If a farmer got there first you often brought them back. We used to let hikers pitch their tents in our fields for 3d. per night, a loaf was 4d. They came from Manchester and bought eggs from us and milk. We made our own butter and cheese. Nothing tastes the same today. Bacon was worth eating, did not stick to the pan, but plenty of fat came out to fry eggs.

Farmers used to set on about four to six men to dig field after field of potatoes. Their wives and children used to pick them and sort them out, the small ones for pigs and the large ones to sell. Besides picking them before school, after school we would call in the fields and pick them till 6 or 7 p.m. They were long days and we were glad when potato-picking time was over. My brother used to pull turnips and sugar beet – pulling them up with frost on, early in the morning, and topping and tailing them.

There were no cars where we lived and we never saw a plane, just heard the curlews and grouse, etc. The ducks used to lay their eggs in the flooded fields and when I was twelve I used to get up at 6 a.m. to go and collect half a bucket full of duck eggs, feed the rabbits and ferrets and then myself, and off to school. Sometimes the ducks got wild and flew away and the keepers would shoot them and give them to mother. Sometimes they would not come home for weeks until the floods went down. Then one duck did not come one night; she went missing for a week. I followed the river and saw our ducks in a cluster. I thought they were talking to our missing duck. I investigated and there was the duck. She had made a beautiful nest and was sitting on eggs. She flew at me but we took her and her eggs home. I have never seen such a nest so deep down at the root of a tree, smothered with rushes.

One day my brother was ploughing with horses when the boss came along and smacked the horses and they ran. He said to my brother, 'That's my speed.' My brother said nothing but thought to himself, 'Come the weekend when I get paid I will show him my speed.' He left and he did not go back. The farmers had iron bars up the windows in those days to stop the boys escaping or doing a 'moonlight flit' as they called it.

But they were happy days. People were trustworthy, more than they are today. We never locked our door at night; the best days have gone. I would not like to be young today when folk are afraid to go out in the dark, even when no one is there. Sometimes I had more than two-and-a-half miles over fields to walk to catch the bus in the dark. I would take the dog to the bus stop and give him a biscuit and send him home. In the end he got tired and refused to come for he was getting old.

Men worked long hours on farms in those days. My brother got £15 a year, paid once a year. But everyone seemed more carefree in those days. They were good days never to return, but I live them over and over again. Life on the farm was a healthy life with plenty of fresh air. The horses did the work and we did everything the hard way as we had no tractors in those days. We helped to stack the sheaves of corn after coming out of school, in little haycocks dotted all over the field.

There are no days to me like my life before I was twenty. I knew no worry. Today they are wanting to forget life by taking drugs before they are twenty. Work keeps your mind off bad things because you are doing a job worth doing and it is satisfying to know it is a worthy job well done. We used to grind our own corn and pulp our own turnips for the cows. I think life was much the same all over England on farms although it is harder work in the hills with dry-walling and sheep jumping over and knocking them down again. We lived two-and-a-half miles from the Pennines. Our cows were fed, brought up and milked by 6.30 a.m. as we used to catch the horse and put the churns in the float, then take it over rough boulders on a tiny cart road for nearly a mile to get to the stage where all the farmers met the milk wagon. The driver of the wagon couldn't get up these hills and narrow lanes with his big wagon by 7 a.m. and ours was his first call.

CHAPTER THIRTEEN

LIFE ON A FARM ON THE ISLE OF WIGHT

Mrs Ann Cheek told us about her life on the Isle of Wight.

I was born in October 1914, the second of five children, in the village of Whitwell on the Isle of Wight, in a small cottage. My father was the driver of a traction engine, driven by steam, hauling a threshing machine round to the various island farms. A large leather belt was fitted between the two machines to drive the threshing machine. My mother told me, years later, that once this belt flew off while in action and father was struck in the face, injuring his face and nose.

When I was three months old, Dad obtained a similar job in the town of Newport, so we had to leave our country cottage and move to the town. This meant Dad had to cycle many miles to some farms, especially if the thresher was at one place for several days at a time. As he was out early in the mornings until late at night, he often had to use a lamp on the bike. This was a carbide lamp. Carbide was placed in the lower container of the lamp and was then drip-fed with water from the upper container and the gas, then formed, passed through a rubber tube to the lamp burner itself.

When I was ten, my Dad died after an operation to his nose,

159

possibly due to the blow I mentioned. My mother nursed him for a year after the operation. His death was a terrible loss to us all and meant a struggle for mother, with five of us children to keep. A widow's pension I think was 10s., with 5s. for the eldest child while still at school and 3s. for any other children. The rent was about 7s. 6d. and a hundredweight of coal was 2s. 6d.

Our various aunts and uncles from the country took it in turn to visit us, bringing vegetables from their gardens. They often gave us children pennies and mine usually went into a tin to save for our School Boot Club. This we had to take to school on Monday mornings and when we had saved enough, we took a card with the amount on to the shoe shop and so had new footwear. In those days they cost about 5s. or 6s. 11d. a pair.

Within three years of Father's death, Mother had to go into hospital for major surgery and by the spring of 1930 it was obvious that she was getting much worse and in that June, passed on, leaving us orphans. We were then scattered around our various relatives.

After our home was disposed of and we, as a family, were all scattered, I went to live with my aunt and uncle in Merstone, a remote village on the island, with no church, no public house, no shop, no electricity and no tap water. My aunt and uncle, who had no children of their own, lived in a semi-detached tied cottage which belonged to the farmer who employed Uncle. I was only fifteen years old and had no other choice, and yet as I look back they were happy days, apart from missing Mum and my family.

I would get up in the morning to see my aunt busy doing the kitchen range while the kettle was boiling on what was called a Beatrice, which was a double-burner paraffin stove. I had to wash downstairs in the kitchen sink, an old earthenware type, with a large block of Watsons soap, which stood in a saucer and, unless the water was very dirty in the bowl, I was told to leave it for Auntie to wash in, as every drop had to be drawn up from a deep well which stood between the two houses.

The bread for breakfast was also kept in a big earthenware type of bin with a heavy lid. Also pork was salted down in a similar bin, for Uncle always kept pigs and I remember how I disliked the first pig-killing day. It was strung up on a pole out in the air, while Auntie made the chitterlings, etc.: but the liver was very nice.

Wash-days were really hard, with all the water to be got from the well, and on a frosty or snowy day one can imagine it all. The copper had to be lit by what Uncle called 'furze stems' and the clothes all pushed down with a copper-stick. Also outside was a very heavy mangle and after all that the copper had to be emptied by hand. In the summer all the washing water was saved to water the plants in the garden.

Paraffin lamps had to be filled every day and I don't know how I did any sewing by that light. I went to bed with a candle and we lit one candle off of the other to save matches. Going out at night was a job till I got used to it, as on a dark night one just groped one's way, unless we carried a hurricane lamp!

There were no fridges, of course, so in the summer our butter went down the well in the bucket to try and keep it firm. I used to have to take an enamel can down into the village to get our milk. The lid of these cans was like a drinking cup.

The day started early in this farming village, as Uncle had to be at work at seven and we could tell the time of day, as at 7.30 a.m. the horse and van came up on the way to the station with milk in churns on its way to the mainland. Horses by then were going into the fields to start work, either ploughing, rolling or harrowing, whichever the season was.

As the years passed, I in turn met and married a farmer's son and I had to get used to having his breakfast ready by 6.30 a.m. and then by 9.30 being out in the fields with his 'Nemmet' [a snack or packed lunch usually eaten mid-morning] as landworkers called it. Summers were the busy time with haymaking and corn cutting and we women would ride into the fields in the wagons and often help, especially by standing up the stooks of corn. My husband also drove the binder, for cutting the corn, with two horses.

Show time was interesting, when the farm horses and wagon went off the 5 miles into Newport with all the brasses shining and the bells rattling. On these mornings we were up by 4 o'clock to get the horses' manes and tails plaited and hoping that it would be fine, and that they would come home with a red rosette. Market Day, too, was a busy time, when pigs and fowls went off to Newport Market and eggs cleaned and sent in to sell. We women sometimes went in by train to see how the pigs sold. Sugar beet time was always busy when the beet went to the station siding in the wagons and then on over to the mainland.

There were not a lot of means of going far in those days and with no other interests for the men, several of them used to go down to the horse stables in the evenings and yarn as my husband racked the horses up for the night. As this was his job, I only saw him one night in the week while we were courting, and that entailed going for a walk round the lanes for an hour and back.

Money wasn't plentiful as we only had 30s. a week and 1 pint of milk a day because he worked on Sundays. On that money we brought up a son, still with no lighting but paraffin and no water. In fact, I was forty-six before we moved and had electricity, and even now I have a brother-in-law still living in that area without water or electricity.

CHAPTER FOURTEEN

A Country Dressmaker

This contribution is reconstructed from an interview with Miss N. Bellamy. Dressmaking was an important job open to girls in the early years of the twentieth century. Miss Bellamy has interesting memories of her training for the job and of the life of the times in the country town of Wisbech in Cambridgeshire.

I started dressmaking in 1906. I was fourteen-and-a-half when I went to work for people named Bellairs on the market place. Next to it was a shop that was a general grocers and drapers and there were always seats by the counter for the customers to sit on and the floor was covered with fresh sawdust each day. Most shops in those days had their floors covered with sawdust, especially butcher's shops.

I was apprenticed there as a dressmaker and as I was the last one to join the firm I came in for all the picking up of pins and searching for patterns. The shop was in a back alley in Sugartub Lane. We had one hefty wench there who came from Smeeth Road. I think she used to come up on the train; she fell down and she nearly knocked the stairs to pieces.

I started in January and I walked from Elm Low Road, opposite the Standard Inn, and I had to walk to and fro for my meals. Each workroom had so many tables and no one made a complete garment. Each table was known as 'skirts' or 'bodice' or 'coats'. We had a head skirt and an assistant skirt, maybe an improver, and one, if not two, apprentices. There was a 'sleeve' table but not so many there; she only made sleeves, and the others only made skirts. There would be 'bodices' or 'tops' and there there was a full gang. There were skirts, bodices, sleeves, jackets, costume jackets and big coats and when the head hand went down to fit a dress (we were upstairs) one of us went with her and held the pins – that is how we learnt to fit. I think it was Mondays and Wednesdays that we apprentices had to get out a stack of patterns, which meant that when a fitting was completed, the pattern was taken off and rolled up and kept so we had to fit it without pins.

The patterns weren't made of paper at first. The original fitting was made up of Holland, a type of linen fabric. That was corrected and that pattern was kept. We had to wash those out and then iron them dry or dry them in front of the fire – that was the apprentice's job. When the cleaner went in, in the morning, she swept the floor and picked all the big pieces out, and the dust was left with the pins in the dustbin. We had to take that right down to the cellar, two flights of stairs, and blow the dirt off and shake these pins till they were clean and put them in a tin or dish.

I worked from eight o'clock in the morning until eight at night and had Wednesday afternoon off. We had dinner hour from one till two and I used to walk down to New Common Bridge and have my dinner and walk back in that hour. When it was very dark and there wasn't much work, we used to leave off at 6 o'clock. Now there must be something in this. I remember distinctly on St Valentine's Day, I could look up at St Peter's Church clock and it would be just a little after six but you can't now. It is darker at 6 o'clock.

I earned 1s. a week. That next year I worked the same hours for 2s. a week and after that I became an improver and I earned 3s. 6d. a week. As an improver they trusted me more to make bindings and stitch them together or have them stitched together and then press them. I could pin coat linings in but I had to sew them in the wrong way – to my idea, I had always sewn this way, left-handed, but this I had to sew that way. The head dressmaker and I hated each other like poison but she did say once, 'I'll give Miss Bellamy her due, but she is the best one to find patterns I've ever had', and I took that as a compliment. She used to say, 'Improve your mind, Miss Bellamy, you are most unintelligent.'

When I worked, all the bodices were boned and they were all hand stitched and the skirts were made with a hook and eye that hooked onto a belt inside this bodice (at the waistline). They all wore long skirts and we put up our hair into plaits and felt our-selves very grown-up. The skirts were just off the ground and the edges were bound with braid so that they didn't wear thin. We used to take it in turns to go down and hand in the keys. And we were also taught how to sit.

They had a big stove like we had at school and the porter got the fire going before we went in at 8 o'clock. He also left two large buckets of coal so we had to keep the fire going. We also had to take the kettle down to the cellars and fill it with water for our head hand's afternoon tea. So we learned by watching and I wish I had stopped there now because she was a good teacher. She had a trick of picking on me and she would sniff and say, 'Miss Bellamy, cultivate your memory.' I often thought to myself, 'I'll cultivate you yet', and one day I got the pip. I stood up, took my pinny off, shook it, folded it, put it on my arm and marched out.

I then went to a private dressmaker. It was a very well-run busi-ness. No one did any other work than their table. There was a table for bodices. The fittings were made, it was patterned and stitched up, and the bodices were always cut at the top, in little pin-tucks. It was put on a lining and we had to oversew the edges and press them flat and then we stitched the bones in. If it was a very nice and well-off person, the bones were stitched in by hand in silk binding, but if it was somebody cheap they had a worsted binding. A belt was stitched on then on the inside of the bodice and the skirt had the eyes on the outside of the skirt band, so that they were hooked in to keep the bodice down. The final fitting was something to be believed: if it was just a little too big or a little too tight, that had to be taken up and undone and remade. It was the same with sleeves: the sleeves had to be made to fit the armhole, so very often there was a good piece to take up, about an inch. With coats I had to learn to press facings, how to cross the material and press the facing and if it needed it, if it was a circular skirt, we had to stretch the lower edge with the flashings. The coat lining was all pinned in first and I started at the wrong end at the top, and worked down to the hem, or so I thought, but I was very soon checked on and I had to hem from the hem upwards.

I lived out of town with my grandmother and we only came into town on Saturdays. She used to wear a shawl and when the weather was cold and bad I used to walk under it, beside her and she used to spread it around us. I had what was taken for asthma when I was a small girl about nine but my grandmother used to say, 'What's good enough for me to suffer from is good enough for my grand-daughter', so I used to have a couple of slices of cold salt pork and some roast potatoes and a glass of stout to go to bed on. Very often I couldn't lie down in bed but as I grew up, I lost that.

I don't think I really saw anything exciting. The only thing I can remember is the lighters on the old canal. They brought the lighters loaded with stones, cobblestones and those sharp, pointed pieces of granite or something like that. They were emptied by the side of the canal or brought further up to Collett's Brickyard. Collett's owned most of these barges. An old horse used to walk on one side of the canal with the rope fixed round his hide and he plodded along, not rushing mind you, but quite quietly. There was always plenty of water in the canal or they could drain it – there was a sluice-gate on the Horsefair on the old canal. When the river was high and they needed more water in the canal, which went as far as Outwell I think or beyond that, they opened the sluice.

On May Day we had sports on the Horsefair. We had several tables and all the school kids had a bonfire and fireworks. There was a greasy pole and men racing towards each other on this greasy pole with a pillow – they had a pillow fight. There were races and all that sort of thing. We were very pleased with that.

I know the fire brigade was summoned by a bomb exploding on the South Brink outside the old police station. [I think she means a maroon – a small explosive charge which was often used as a signal.] We once had a Wild West Show. What is now one side of Queens Road was a huge meadow and they had that for a week; they had horses and heavens knows what.

I remember one Christmas, a gang of our young bloods discovered a slide outside what was known as Howletts Hill where the bus service had a huge bus station. There was a doctor's surgery opposite the Flower Pot and they started a wide slide, about twenty of them. They made that slide down along Elm Road over Elm Bridge and Elm High Road and joined up on the same slide and it was like glass.

I can remember the lamplighter – must be a few years back. He had a long pole with a hook on it. The gas bracket had a chain with a loop and the hook went through the loop and pulled the gas on. He went round early next morning and switched them off. I suppose they had a pilot light in them to light them or they had a pilot light on top of the pole with a special lever. But the lights were very few and far between.

In my leisure time I used to sew or read. I used to work on Saturdays until 9 o'clock in the evening, so being near the Market Place we used to hear the Salvation Army as they used to turn up there.

The first Pension and Dole Office was a little business on the river bank. It was a wood merchant's office in those days and then, I think, it moved over to a tin place in Alexander Road. It was a little tin office of some kind. I think it may have been St Peter's Church Hall. There was a pub on the Nene Parade where there was a dole office but, of course, that wasn't thought of when I was an improver. When I was seventeen, then this National Health came up and at my age we were most indignant we had to pay 4d. for this insurance and we all moaned and said, 'That is 1 lb of sweets less for us. It is not fair.'

Women around here have always worked on the land. Of course, people always had a pig in a sty and a few chickens in the back yard run.

You could go to London on a Sunday afternoon for about 7s. 6d. and have a few hours there. The telephone was a great thing with us, and I can remember that being installed with a huge ear-piece.

We attended church or chapel, whichever offered us the most. I was christened in St Augustine's Church and so was my sister. She was married there. I was godmother to her children there.

They must have been very hard-up then, very poor, because I have heard my family talk about the first soup kitchen. It was somewhere in the Church Mews and it was a little kitchen, I suppose, and the man made the soup the day before. At night he put the copper lid off and when he went next day to heat the soup, and wash and scrub the floor, there was a black cat dead in the soup, so he picked it out and wrapped it up and hid it. The Mayor with the Corporation opened it and was given the first taste of soup. He said it was the most delicious soup he had ever tasted and at that moment a little old lady came in wringing her hands and saying, 'Has anybody seen my black cat? He is lost. I can't find him.' She didn't know he was wrapped up behind us.

When we were children we never told each other we were bringing our whips and tops. Somebody brought a whip and top to school and we all followed suit. The same with the hoops. Do you remember those big hoops? Some of them had an iron hoop with an iron hook to it. They used to make wooden hoops as well. We used to chalk a pattern on the top of our hoop in different colours. You could see the colours flashing as it went round. We had picture books with pictures you cut out or scraps and then put them in a book with a handle; things were pushed in the back of the book in the spine and you picked one out – a sort of game of chance. Then we had skipping ropes and balls to play with.

When you look back and picture the fields early on a summer's day, a mass of buttercups and daisies and the hedges were masses of wild roses in May, they smelled lovely. You might get the smell of somebody's pigsty thrown in for luck!

We didn't have time for hobbies because most of us were working from eight in the morning until eight at night. As we grew up we went dancing or riding bicycles. Our women, they always worked on the land and when a squad of city girls came here as the Womens' Land Army, we laughed. They wore khaki suits and puttees, heavy soled boots – and we laughed at them.

Our dancing cost us about 1s. 6d. an evening and we had a fiddler and a piano, and a piper. We made a lot of our own entertainment. We had the pictures and they were silent in those days. There was someone playing the piano while the film was on. The seats were uncomfortable. My father, having a barber's shop, he always had the posters so he got two free tickets, but I don't think he ever went.

There was the old Hippodrome and they had music hall acts there. And there was a picture house where the Onyx was built but that was burned down. There were very funny films there – there was murder and heavens knows what and the victim was always bound to the railway track; it always stopped as the engine neared. It looked as if it was going to cut her head off! We had Charlie Chaplin and we thought he was wonderful. There was Fatty Arbuckle, Harold Lloyd and yet they would seem tame now, wouldn't they? If my mother and I went together, it never failed: we would just get settled and either the last of the fire brigade or somebody else, a sweep perhaps, would have to come by and we would all have to stand in a row and miss the most vital parts of the picture.

When the fruit picking started the Londoners used to come here and the farm lorries would meet them at the station. They would

169

provide them with sacks of oats or straw to sleep on. Then the students used to come from Cambridge and they would go round taking orders. They would buy their bread or their meat or whatever they wanted. Young doctors and nurses, they would come and look after the babies while the parents worked. They earned quite good money and at the weekends they were bouncing for joy. They would get drunk and fight.

I think the children had a far better time – they had a home life. We were poor but then everybody was, nearly everybody. We made our own entertainment, we used to read or sew.

I can remember the Suffragette Movement and joined it myself. I screamed 'Votes for Women' with the best of them. I went to Selwyn Hall to a meeting. That hall has since been pulled down to build some offices which later became the Conservative Club in Alexander Road. It has been used like the Town Hall. At that meeting it was the first time I had ever been in the arms of the law.

There is a legend that somewhere outside the Rising Sun, the pub at Leverington, a black dog used to join a lonely walker and escort him harmless to the top of Sutton Bridge and then vanish. I had a friend living next door but one to the Sun and I used to go down there every week in the winter but I never saw the black dog.

CHAPTER FIFTEEN

At the End of the Day

Before drawing this work to a conclusion there are a number of points, made more briefly by other correspondents, that help to round off the picture of the lives of country women in the first half of the twentieth century.

The way in which young girls were expected to help out on the farm was pointedly described by Mrs A. Borrett who spent her childhood on her grandmother's farm at Depwade in Norfolk. 'Before going to school,' she said, 'I got up at five in the morning, getting Grandma's twenty-five milk cows up to be milked. They knew the bay they had to go into, there was no muddle. They came one by one and found their food in the trough in front of them. Then I went to the field to feed the hens, the ducks and the tame rabbits. I went then with the horseman to feed the horses and take them down to the pond to drink. Sometimes we had to break the ice on the pond in winter. Then I went on to the lambing pens to look at the expectant ewes. Yes, we had a full day. But we were well fed, going home from school to a hot rabbit pie and dumplings followed by a big treacle syrup pudding or currant duff.'

Mrs Borrett went on to describe, 'The wonderful days between the wars, when you could walk for miles and miles seeing rabbits, brown squirrels, dormice nesting in the corn and the game springing up, the deer, the birds and hardly a farmer's gun. There were no chemicals to kill the plants, no poison put down to kill the wildlife.

Today, I walk the public footpaths through streams of rubbish. We could walk the footpaths and still have clean shoes and white stockings. Now we have to wear high rubber Wellingtons and chance our luck on our walks.' Reverting to social change she pointed out, 'Today all the friendliness, the togetherness, the love and understanding have gone out of the world. As a young girl I went round to the elderly people with sacks of wood and coal from my uncle's coal yard. We looked after our grandmas, grandads and other people. Now that has all gone. The old age pensioners are mugged, the children get sexually assaulted and the animals cruelly treated.' Her sentiments are echoed by many people of her generation.

I shall now turn to some information from Mrs Sheila Graver from Wrexham, Clwyd, who described how her mother went into domestic service. She said, 'From an early age, probably about eleven, my mother worked at weekends and holidays at a farm where her grandparents worked. She helped indoors and outdoors. When she left school at fourteen (in 1926) she went to live in at the same farm. The farmer's wife expected it and my mother liked the farmer and his wife; they treated her well. My mother had her own little room at the back of the house. She received 4s. a week to start with; after four years this rose to 5s. The only time off was from 1.30 p.m. to 5 p.m. on a Saturday. She always had to be back for milking. My mother did all kinds of work: milking, fed animals, made hay, washed, cleaned and did many other jobs. Of course, there was no electricity in the house. Now and then she went in the pony and float to town, either to Wrexham or Ellesmere. She saved £4 over a long time to buy a bicycle. This gave her a little freedom.

'When she was seventeen, she went as a vessel maid to another farm. It was a cheesemaking farm and there was far more work to do, and more workers were employed. She was not happy; the other girls were rude and rather coarse. She received 12s. a week.

'After two years she left and went to another farm nearby for 14s. a week. The work was similar but cheese was only made if milk was returned from the dairy. The farmer made the milk into cheese. After a while she went to another farm where she did indoor and outdoor work for £1 a week. Here the farmer made advances to the maids, so she left and returned to her first place of work.

'In 1933 she got married and continued to work on odd days for her old boss and also for the farmer's wife at the place where my father worked.

'She also helped run the smallholding with my father, where they lived with an old man. When the old man died they were given the tenancy.'

The extent to which women worked on the farm seems to have varied in different parts of the country as may be seen in earlier chapters.

Mrs Ann Powers (my wife's sister) lived in the Fen country of west Norfolk and says, 'At the beginning of the century women would not have a lot of time to work on the land. Cooking, washing and cleaning occupied most of their days. Apart from the large families of the time, often the single farm labourers would live in the farmhouse with the family. There would be none of the modern conveniences; cooking would be done on the large black-leaded ranges. Soap and soda would be the only cleaning materials – none of the modern detergents. The farmer's wife would keep a few hens and sell the eggs to supplement the housekeeping money. At Christmas she would rear poultry, ducks and geese to sell.

'A sheep-farmer's wife would have to help at lambing-time. The lambs would probably be bottle-fed every few hours and the really weak ones warmed in the ovens to help them to survive. Some farmers kept a few cows for household use and the surplus milk would be sold locally. Some people made butter. The milk was separated each day by pouring it into a bowl on top of a separator. This had a bell which rang when the speed got to sixty turns a minute, cranking by hand. Then the cream was turned into an earthenware jar called a pipkin and the separated milk drained into another pot to be used to feed young calves and other animals. The cream was put into a churn once a week. This was turned by hand, using a cranking handle until it thickened into butter. When ready, the lumps of butter were cut up and patted into weights on slate slabs. There were no fridges, so if the weather was hot the butter would be kept cool by lowering it into a well until it was fetched by the local grocer. Often the butter and eggs were taken to a local town on market day to be sold to the stallholders.

'After harvest the women would go out to the fields to glean. This was collecting any fallen grain or stems of corn to be used to feed the poultry.'

Women's pay was poor. Miss Brett from Diss, Norfolk, told me, 'I worked in greenhouses in the early 1930s when I was fifteen years old and my average wage was 10s. for a fifty-hour week. When I left at the age of twenty-two in 1938, my take-home pay was £1 6s. I had a box to put money for clothes, presents and savings and a little was given to my parents. There wasn't the money for holidays unless you went to stay with relatives or friends, but what we had never had we didn't expect.'

Only three of the persons contacted were able to give me any personal account of life in the Women's Land Army and two of these consisted of published material. Violet Cowley sent a copy of her autobiography *Over My Shoulder*. Mr Albert Poulter of Witham, Essex, sent me a copy of a small book he had edited and published in 1987. It was entitled *Reminiscences of a Land Girl* and had been written by Marjorie Geere in 1941. Both these describe conditions during the Second World War. I do not propose to reprint material from these books but recommend them to readers who are interested in more detail in the work of women in the Land Army.

The Women's Land Army had been formed during the First World War. There was a shortage of labour for many young men were leaving the land to join the armed forces. By 1917 the situation had become desperate and it was said that only about three

Members of the Women's Land Army during the First World War

weeks' food supply was left in the country when the Minister of Agriculture, Richard Protheroe, decided to establish the Land Army. Under the directorship of Dame Meriel Talbot, women were recruited from the towns, as well as the countryside, and by the end of the War about 23,000 had enrolled in the organization.

While I have no direct account of life in the Land Army during the First World War, Mrs S. Dobson of Lythe, near Whitby, in North Yorkshire, has sent some photographs of friends of her mother who served during that period.

The Land Army was re-formed on 1 June 1939 in anticipation of the approaching War, so that there were already about 1,000 girls trained and ready to go into action on the farms when war broke out on 1 September that year. By 1943, 80,000 had enrolled. Thus the Land Army played a much greater role in the Second World War.

Land girls were employed in all the tasks on the farm. Some were also engaged in horticulture and others in forestry. They came from all sections of society and some of the town girls had difficulty in adapting to country life. While many of the girls were employed by individual farmers, over 26,000 were employed by the County War Agricultural Committees. These workers constituted a mobile force that could be sent anywhere within the county. Many of them were accommodated in Women's Land Army hostels, of which there were 690 by January 1944, 475 of which were run by the Land Army. Others were run by the Young Women's Christian Association or by the War Agricultural Executive Committees. The accommodation varied from manor houses to converted chicken houses. Those in private employment were usually billeted with private residents in the village where they worked.

The Land Army even had its own song, 'Back to the Land', the words and music being composed by land girls P. Adkins and E.K. Loring.

Back to the land, we must all lend a hand
To the farms and the fields we must go.
There's a lot to be done,
Though we can't fire a gun,
We still do our bit with the hoe.
When your muscles are strong,
You will soon get along
And you'll think that a country life's grand.
We're all needed now.
We must all speed the plough.
So come with us – back to the land.

Mrs I. Anderson of Ketton, Stamford, Lincolnshire, recalled a few 'happenings' when she was a land army girl. She says, 'I was employed by the Leicester and Rutland War Agricultural Committee for the first eighteen months or so and four of us used to cycle around together to whichever farmer needed us. On our first day we had to go to the kennels of the Quorn Hunt and our introduction to farm work was to shovel piles of dog mess onto trailers for the men to spread. Talk about pong – it was worse than pigs – and we had to eat our sandwiches without even being able to wash our hands!

'The next day we were clearing a straw stack and, of course, as it came to the bottom, we were having to stab rats and mice (and poor baby bunny rabbits) with our pitchforks. I was merrily scratching away when I felt something tickling my knee. I rubbed it and it moved upwards. By this time I was jumping up and down and eventually a little mouse came up my arm and popped out of the neck of my pullover! We new girls realized then why the men all had their trousers tied up with string around their knees! And we also tucked the bottom of our trousers into our boots!

'Another time, we were doing some threshing (a team of four of us used to follow the drum). One miserable day in October we were threshing in a field next to an airfield, which is now the East Midlands Airport. We worked all morning, then went up to the barn to eat our lunch because it was too cold to sit outside. While we were eating, the leader of the gang looked out of the door and realized that the wind had changed because the smoke from the piled-up chaff, which we had to burn, was blowing the opposite way from where we'd left it. The wind had changed in those few minutes and it was enough to have set fire to the corn stack and the straw stack and the threshing drum in between. So we had to spend the rest of the day fighting the fire, saving the stacks of corn we'd already threshed and moving the remaining straw and corn before everything was ruined. In the end, some fire fighters from the air-field came over and doused it all with foam – and that was that. Our leader got a rocket, of course, and when we got a new drum we always made sure that someone was left by the chaff fire to make sure the same thing didn't happen again! Awful job, threshing, especially in the depths of winter. We followed the drum from about September through to April and the only time we didn't thresh was when there was too much snow for us to cycle through to the farms. Then they used to put us on to shovelling snow from the streets of Loughborough.

'It was a much easier life when I was transferred to the Hunts, Cambs, and Ely District and lived at home, just cycling the short journey to Wisbech St Mary, every day to work on Allan Hudson's fruit farm, hoeing and pruning in winter and fruit picking in summer. Lovely! But I wouldn't want to do it all again.'

The Women's Institute (WI) movement has played an important part in the social side of the countryside since its formation in 1917. During the period in which we are interested, the movement grew rapidly so that by the time of the Second World War, there were institutes in the great majority of the villages, with a membership of some 300,000.

The institutes were established with three aims: to instruct, to interest and to amuse and they proceeded to pursue these objectives with vigour. Experts were brought in to instruct women on the most efficient methods of home-making and the management of their limited financial resources. Demonstrations on cooking and food preservation, on gardening and on crafts such as weaving, basketmaking and dressmaking were frequently part of their activities. In many country towns the Women's Institutes organized stalls in the local markets on which they sold produce grown or made by their members.

While remaining non-political, they encouraged their members to take an active interest in local government and to be involved in the social life of their communities. In many areas they brought pressure to bear on local authorities for the improvement of social amenities, such as the collection and disposal of refuse, the provision of water, gas and electricity services, and the extension of bus services and the provision of public telephones.

As far as the entertainment side of their activities was concerned, they often organized dramatic activities, revived country dancing as well as holding dances and social events of many kinds, including fêtes and country fairs.

The membership seemed to have been representative of all classes of society and they provided an important meeting place for the women of the village. They were also able to represent women's points of view and promote their interests.

While the Womens' Institutes were non-sectarian, the churches often had their own women's organizations. The Church of England was represented by the Mothers' Union while the non-conformist chapels also had women's groups. Women were also involved in the organization of the village halls that were opened in many places during this period and in such youth organizations as the Girl Guides and the Girls' Brigade as well as the Cubs and Boy Scouts groups.

In some places the British Legion had women members and women helpers and everywhere they were involved in helping with many of the men's activities such as the cricket club, where they would provide refreshment for players and spectators. It seems that it was only the Friendly Societies from which they were excluded.

Many village shops were run by women and it was not uncommon to find the postal services were also supplied by a woman. While most farms were run by men, there were some women who owned and ran their own farms.

While life was hard, most of the elderly ladies I have contacted have happy memories of their early years. These memories centre round their families and the friendships they encountered in the village communities in which they lived. Most of them feel that the quality of life has decreased, that the ties of family and community are no longer so strong and that while people are no doubt better off financially and materially, they no longer enjoy the peace, quiet and contentment that seem (at least in retrospect) to have characterized life in the period before the Second World War.

One thing that is evident is that material possessions do not in themselves give happiness. If they did, no doubt we should be a great deal happier than any previous generation. There is no evidence that we are. There is truth in the words of one contributor, 'What you have never had, you don't miss.' We might be unhappy if we lost our televisions and cars but previous generations seem to have been happy without them.

There is no doubt that women's lives have improved in that in many of the tasks around the home they are aided by modern machines, but has this improved their social status or their general satisfaction with life? This is not a question that can be answered here but I have no doubt readers will reach their own conclusions.

FURTHER READING

Blomefield, Marthena,   *The Bullymunge Pit* and *Nuts in the Rookery*, Faber, London, 1946
Bow Nets and Water Lilies, Faber, London, 1948

Brooke, Justin and Edith, *Suffolk Prospect*, Faber, London, 1963

Cowley, Violet,   *Over My Shoulder*, Stockwell, Ilfracombe, 1985

Geere, Marjorie,   *Reminiscences of a Land Girl in Witham*, A. Poulter, Witham, Essex, 1987

Hales, Jane,   *One Thing and Another*, C. Veal, Wisbech, 1982

Harris, Mollie,   *Cotswold Privies*, Chatto and Windus, London, 1984
From Acre End, Chatto and Windus, London, 1986

Haworth, Josephine,   *The Country Habit*, Methuen, London, 1987

Hill, Susan,   *The Magic Apple Tree: A Country Year*, Hamish Hamilton, London, 1982

MacArthur-Onslow, Annette,   *Round Houses*, Collins, London, 1975

Megginson, Irene,   *Mud on my Doorstep: Reminiscences of a Yorkshire Farmwife*, Hutton Press, Beverley, 1987

'Read, Miss',   *Chronicles of Fairacre*, Michael Joseph, London, 1964

Reeves, Marjorie,   *Sheep Bell and Ploughshare*, Granada, London, 1980

Sackville-West, V.   *The Women's Land Army*, Michael Joseph, London, 1944

Stewart, Sheila,   *Lifting the Latch: A Life on the Land*, Oxford University Press, 1988

Thompson, Flora,   *Lark Rise to Candleford*, Oxford University Press, 1945
Peverill Papers, Century, London, 1986

Uttley, Alison,   *The Country Child*, Faber, London, 1931
Country Things, Faber, London, 1946

Wells, Irene,   *My Life in the Land Army*, I. Wells, Alcester, Warwickshire, 1984

Whyte, Betsy,   *The Yellow on the Broom*, Chambers, Edinburgh, 1979